COLLABORATIVE LEADERSHIP FOR CLASSROOM AND SCHOOL

COLLABORATIVE LEADERSHIP FOR CLASSROOM AND SCHOOL

DON BROADWELL

Collaborative Leadership for Classroom and School

iUniverse books may be ordered through booksellers or by contacting:

iUniverse
1663 Liberty Drive
Bloomington, IN 47403
www.iuniverse.com
1-800-Authors (1-800-288-4677)

Because of the dynamic nature of the Internet, any web addresses or links contained in this book may have changed since publication and may no longer be valid. The views expressed in this work are solely those of the author and do not necessarily reflect the views of the publisher, and the publisher hereby disclaims any responsibility for them.

Any people depicted in stock imagery provided by Thinkstock are models, and such images are being used for illustrative purposes only. Certain stock imagery © Thinkstock.

ISBN: 978-1-5320-0907-5 (sc)
ISBN: 978-1-5320-0908-2 (e)

Library of Congress Control Number: 2016918863

Print information available on the last page.

iUniverse rev. date: 11/22/2016

To the millions of US teachers who, despite the furor going on around their profession, close that classroom door and begin the wonderfully tedious task of preparing children for their uniquely interactive futures.

I'd also like to give a special dedication to Major General O. K. Steele (Retired) of the US Marine Corps and to the memory of Dr. Thomas Gordon of Gordon Training International.

CONTENTS

PREFACE

Following six years in the Marines, I spent four decades in schools. By the fall of 2010, I was pleasantly retired, playing golf on occasion, and not expecting to conduct another weekend workshop or sit at a keyboard to write. For keeping busy, for pocket change, and for the company of young people, I delivered pizza on the weekends.

One day, on a whim, I googled "Collaboration—Obama," and I came across a *USA Today* article entitled "Obama Bets on Collaboration." That got my attention. I had taught collaborative leadership to classroom teachers for the better part of two decades, withdrawing from that field when standardized testing began to dominate the curriculum around 2005.

While teaching at Seattle Pacific University, I'd kept my nine-to-five job supplying library books to Pacific Northwest schools. This placed me in the unique position of taking in the ever-present criticism of education while also having the confidence of librarians, who shared with me their staffs' reactions. As a book rep, I have been education's proverbial fly on the wall, listening and watching as everyone from the US Congress to the Gates Foundation seemed to know more about teaching than the professionals who performed it. I was particularly intrigued when, in the 1990s, under the rubric of "decentralized decision making," collaboration was tried and found wanting. Could a return to collaborative deciding be at hand?

I searched further, my interest growing as I went. At length, I discovered President Obama's flagship initiative on collaboration, the

Open Innovation Portal, and its $650 million program for promising new ideas. After years of arguing for children's voices in classroom decision-making, I had finally found the invitation I sought. After an eight-year thrust toward standardized tests, teacher/student relationship building was on its way back ... or so I thought.

"Participative leading," as educators called it at the time, was in vogue during the Human Potential days of the 1990s. But participation proved to be amorphous, time-consuming, and unproductive. By the year 2000, to no one's surprise, school administrators began to stomp their feet. Top-down leading returned in force. Command and control was once more the accepted modality, at least in practice. Participative decision making gets lip service, but given the time needed for group decision making and the confusion over method—not to mention the apparent absence of accountability—the collapse of "participation" could well have been foreseen. In any event, the time had come for me to dip my toe back in the water. I recreated my nonprofit Collaborative Center and once more commenced to teach.

Leadership in general has undergone more than a few changes since the early days of civilization. Certainly the Industrial Revolution called for a rational, teachable model, and this was provided by Frederick Taylor's *The Principles of Scientific Management*, first published in 1911. However, Taylor overlooked much that the ancients had to offer. More than 2,500 years ago, Lao Tzu wrote, "A leader is best when people barely know he exists." With collaborative leadership promising to move again to the foreground, any contrast between Taylor and Lao Tzu should be welcome. Collaboration—a more descriptive term than *participation*—might be the answer to the Taylor-Tzu debate. As Aristotle might have said, it has become "a likely impossibility to replace an unconvincing possibility" (Anderson, 69).

What exactly does a leader do? Does he drive his people with alpha male demands (the transactional model)? Does she invite workers to share mission and goals (the transformational model)? Does she strive to meet the needs of employees (the servant leader model)? Is there room in our schools for the collaborative model, popularized by Thomas Gordon more than forty years ago in his book *Teacher Effectiveness Training*? Or will a combination of these models prove facile, productive, even beguiling for children and teacher alike?

My first exposure to theories of leadership came under the benevolent auspices of the US Marine Corps some fifty years ago. Following three months of Officer Candidate School and six months of command training, I got my first assignment to lead a platoon in the First Marine Division. After eighteen months of infantry duty, I was moved to the USMC Mountain Warfare Training Center in California's High Sierras. There, along with twelve other guides, I was to train marines in the science of over-snow combat and, during the summer, the practice of cliff assault. The thirty-six marines we trained each month would not be forming a fighting unit in and of themselves. Instead, they were expected to serve as advisers to large-scale missions should warfare break out at high elevations, which it has—just not in 1962.

After several years in the mountains, I bounced between desk jobs for two more years and then took my leave to study theology. My seminary training gave me my first exposure to group decision making, and I have not looked back. I have watched group-process leading (as it was called in the 1960s) morph into conflict resolution, and then into conflict prevention, negotiated leadership, no-lose leading, participatory leading, and now leading via collaboration.

Collaboration is an appropriate description. Today, companies in the tech industry know that ideas can come from every level of the organization. In light of the many exhortations to collaborate, all that is missing is how and when. These are topics I address in this book.

I am indebted to (then Captain) O. K. Steele for showing me

the human side of authority while we were assigned to the Mountain Warfare Center. Among other things, Steele told me to quit demanding that the marines salute me. We were a small unit of only thirteen guides, and, he said, "You never know when you'll need one of our guys to dig you from under a mountain of snow." I took his advice, and I remember the times that came after as the closest of team bonding. They were among the happiest and most challenging of my career.

The day I met Steele, he invited me for a run. As we jogged in the crisp mountain air, he plied me with questions about his new job. Who were these guides he'd be working with? What should he expect from us, and what did we expect from him? He was quick to assure me I'd have a job as his assistant, and soon he placed me in charge of the winter syllabus. Since he was a novice skier, he quickly became my pupil. I was below him in rank, and I revered him for delegating me second in command. My esteem for him has never changed.

From Captain Steele, I learned never to issue an order I could not reasonably expect to enforce. Also, nobody knows how to do the job better than the man who is doing it. Don't tell people how do things, instead tell them what you want done and leave them alone. This advice actually goes to General George Patton, who said, "Never tell people how to do things. Tell them what to do and they will surprise you with their ingenuity." Unlike Patton, who had a reputation for gruffness, Steele carried a gentility that would make *Gone with the Wind*'s Rhett Butler proud. During the two years we worked together, I never heard him raise his voice.

I am determined to emulate Ort Steele as I write this book. I will not raise my voice. There is nothing in this book that one *ought* to do to become a more effective teacher. There are no shoulds, oughts, or musts. There is only invitation. In fact, you will discover you are already more of a leader than you know. Today's teachers live in a hypercritical environment, and that tends to rob them of confidence and make them feel there is little room for mistakes; they must control their classroom and have leadership down pat. But how do they do this without seeming like Genghis Khan at recess? I will address such riddles in the pages ahead. Once more, our understanding of leadership is about to change.

INTRODUCTION

I have yet to meet a young person who liked his or her schooling. In hindsight, school was a compulsive exercise in obedience. As I've said, I'm retired, and I deliver pizzas on the weekends mostly because I enjoy being around young people. It keeps me young myself. What quickly became obvious to me is that most of our young workers got absolutely nothing from their educational experience. After dropping out of high school, most of my young friends completed their high school equivalency; some are even enrolled in our local community college. Others, ambition intact, are studying vocations like computer science, IT, or industrial drafting. These young people all tell me the same thing: high school neither challenged them nor set them free. Uniformly, they were eager to get away, to spread their wings and fly.

There are dim signals that schooling is changing. In Washington State, 2015 Teacher of the Year Lyon Terry is being rewarded for allowing his children more of a voice than he gives himself. Will Terry set a precedent for others to follow? Can we somehow expand the voices of children to a point where they can help determine outcomes in the classroom? What model will teachers adhere to? And what does this have to do with classroom leadership?

My goal is for teachers to model collaborative leading in situations of choice and to share collaborative deciding with their students. *Collaborative Leadership for Classroom and School* follows a developmental approach, meaning I use a building block scheme to add small units to what has already been learned.

Chapter 1 describes the evolution of leadership thinking from Lao Tzu, writing five hundred years before the Christian era, through the 1990s and the Human Potential Movement to the present Obama-inspired emphasis on collaboration. Chapter 2 describes collaboration under the most basic conditions—for example, when there is no anger or hidden agenda. Chapter 3 details how to collaborate amid complications like angry feelings and when stakeholders are not forthcoming.

In chapter 4, I examine *flex leading*—fluid problem solving from a solid base. This is the chapter that reconciles authority and participation so that each is a potential home base for the teacher. The key ingredient here is personal values. The role played by values is spelled out so that there is no doubt that authority and collaboration are both valid starting places for leaders; they exist side by side. Collaboration is only one of many problem-solving options, but it can be the option of first refusal, inviting teachers to shift their leader base away from traditional authority (see appendices 2 and 3).

Chapter 5 looks at generational changes that point to collaboration as the optimal style for today's student. It delivers case studies from a number of teachers who use my model. Chapter 6, the epilogue, explores the political drama unleashed by No Child Left Behind. Former Washington, DC, education commissioner Michelle Rhee maintained that "the civil rights movement didn't work things out by consensus" (Rhee 2010, para. 9), but for school reform in the twenty-first century, I conclude that collaboration is the right choice. In fact, collaboration and school reform will eventually be seen as the same thing.

Teachers will find it easier to shape their classrooms into a problem-solving whole than to be the "sage on the stage," the omniscient decider. Teachers can energize their classrooms, gain buy-in from students, and implement solutions together with their kids. Leading becomes as stress-free an activity as reading a book or eating lunch. In the process, teachers can raise achievement to levels they, and the public, desire.

Collaborative leadership brings challenges. Teachers who use it must adjust the expectations of children who do not immediately understand that it is for special occasions and does not dominate the decision-making process. On occasion, these same teachers must explain to succeeding teachers (those who inherit their class for the following school year) why their children are so vocal. Principals need to understand the method in order to evaluate their staff. Still, teachers who lead with collaboration release the creative energy of their children, gain buy-in from their classrooms, and find implementing decisions quite easy thanks to the commitment of their students. They also have the satisfaction of preparing children for a future vastly different from the one for which they themselves were prepared.

I believe that the terms *leadership* and *problem solving* are interchangeable. In this writing, as in Thomas Gordon's Teacher Effectiveness series, the terms are synonymous. That assumption has proven itself to be true over and over again during my thirty-plus years of teaching collaborative leading, yet the evidence is anecdotal and the time left waiting for empirical proof is short. Only those with the courage of their convictions need to read on.

CHAPTER 1

CHANGING LEADERSHIP:
A BRIEF HISTORY

We now know that along with everything else,
leadership changes.
—Barbara Kellerman

My excursion into the ministry was as brief as it was discouraging. Still, I remember the moment when my leadership style changed forever. As the freshly minted youth pastor of a small New Jersey church, I was tasked with organizing my high school fellowship for a Christmas pageant. Although steeped in authority-based deciding, I had taken a loose rein with my kids during the months prior to the event, placing myself in a listening role more than a directive one. But I longed for a more hands-on opportunity. The idea of thirty youngsters needing a Hollywood-style director captured my imagination; it seemed the perfect chance for me to take charge. I waded in with barrels blazing, giving directions left and right. My kids were confused and upset.

This misadventure ended with the group's president stepping up to me with, "We want you out of here." Years later, I would learn how I could have stayed in character and still met the need for direction among the group. For the moment, however, I was stunned. I was not over it when several youngsters checked to see if I was okay. Since that day, I have learned many more lessons, some of which I actually enjoyed.

This I learned above all else: leadership has always changed, and it continues to do so. In the classroom, strict pedagogy, once embraced, is now shunned. As new methods emerge, teachers give them a try to see if they are effective. In the pages to come, we'll take a look at how leadership in general has changed through the ages. Such a historical perspective can help you understand why and how your leadership methods in the classroom will change over time. A big-picture view is important. So let's dive right in!

From its inception in the pre-Christian era through the mid-twentieth century, leadership's rate of change has been glacial. Over the past fifty years, however, the pace has increased to something vastly more intense. Today, leadership is in a quandary. Training is a $50 billion per year industry (Kellerman 2012, 154), although we are no closer to leadership nirvana than we were previously. "Bottom line: while the leadership industry has been thriving—growing and prospering beyond anyone's early imaginings—leaders by and large are performing poorly, worse in many ways than before" (Kellerman 2012, xv). How to account for this apparent disconnect when, in fact leadership and followership have both evolved over time? Let's start from the beginning.

Leadership: The Ancient's View

From the start of recorded history, kings, princes, and clerics ruled the masses—so much so that by the seventeenth century, philosopher Thomas Hobbes framed life as "solitary, brutish, poor, nasty, and short" (Kellerman 2010, xix). Still, there were leaders concerned with who and how to lead. In the beginning, there were Lao Tzu, Confucius,

Plato, and Plutarch. Confucius, born in 551 BC, believed that those in authority should behave as gentlemen. Self-educated and without a platform from which to officially teach, he organized groups of disciples and taught them the elements of leadership that he embraced.

Confucius was deeply disturbed by the authoritarian conditions of his time, and he dedicated his life to social reform. His *Analects* or teachings, which were compiled by his students after his death, revealed a primary emphasis on sincerity and a commitment to ethical leadership. He advocated that leaders should be older, wiser, and better—in fact, as close to perfection as possible. He taught that "those who wished to secure the good of others have already secured their own" (Anderson 1990, 52). He believed that government should make its end the happiness of its subjects, not the pleasure of its rulers. Confucius has been called perhaps the most influential teacher in the history of the world (Anderson 1990, 50).

Plato, born in 423 BC, was a contemporary of Confucius in focus and in thought, if a century younger by birth. He too believed in the education of leaders and surrounded himself with students at the Academy of Athens, which he founded. In *Republic* 473 c–d, he states that leading is based in wisdom and that unless philosophers rule as kings or kings become philosophers, cities will have no rest from their troubles—nor, he surmised, will the human race. "Confucius's gentleman leader and Plato's philosopher-king have elements in common: they aspire to perfection; they reflect a context that is leader-centric; and they are of a historical moment in which good governance seemed completely to depend on good, even great leadership" (Kellerman 2012, 7).

Through the Middle Ages

The notion of the valiant leader did not begin to wane until 1215, when King John of England was compelled to sign the Magna Carta, admitting that his authority was not absolute and his will could not be arbitrarily put to work. This might have been a benchmark in the history of leadership, but the Great Man theory would not fade easily. It would take another 750 years before scholarship would join reality in promoting gender-neutral leadership and exploring the prospect of leader and follower laboring together to decide.

Change, in other words, was slow. Although the Magna Carta was a watershed in which the king was obliged to succumb to his followers, this was, after all, the Middle Ages, when royalty ruled on earth, along with God through the Catholic Church. It is extraordinary, then, that the most durable, the most secular, the most pragmatic of leadership treatises was Niccolo Machiavelli's *The Prince* (1513). Without at least a casual reading of Machiavelli, one easily falls into a commonplace misunderstanding, using the pejorative term *Machiavellian* to indicate cruelty as a sought-after leadership trait.

In fact, Machiavelli was primarily intent on preserving his principality, keeping peace in the domain, and of course, maintaining his power. "As such, he is grounded in the here and now, does not bow to a moral compass, either religious or otherwise, and his loyalty is to himself and his subjects only" (Kellerman 2012, 9). Machiavelli believed his sojourns into cruelty were necessary based on his lack of faith in the human condition. Followers, to Machiavelli, were "fickle, ungrateful, pretenders and dissemblers, evaders of danger, eager for gain" (Kellerman 2012, 9). This, together with a glut of crises in the Medici reign, made cruelty a viable option. Consequently, Machiavelli believed that a leader should be good, but *willing to be not good*. In any event, Machiavelli viewed cruelty as less abhorrent than a leader's mercy, since "too much mercy allows disorders to continue from which come killings or robberies, activities that hurt the whole community" (Zuckert 2015).

Like Machiavelli, Thomas Hobbes, whose *Leviathan* (1651) followed *The Prince* by a little over a century, was concerned with how to keep order in a disorderly world. Both found followers untrustworthy; they were fearful, rapacious, selfish, and dangerous. Hobbes argued for an authoritarian, even a totalitarian ruler (the leviathan of his title). Yet unlike Machiavelli, Hobbes turned his attention from those in power to those without power. His focus became followers' rights, specifically the right to a quality life.

For Hobbes, life under medieval rule was, as mentioned earlier, solitary, poor, nasty, brutish, and short. The life expectancy for males during Hobbes's era was forty-three years (Woodbury 2014, para. 3). The sea change he provoked was to make at least one right of ordinary people superior to any right of their king: the right to life. "The change from an orientation by natural duties to an orientation by natural rights finds its most potent expression in the ideas of Hobbes, who put the unconditional right to life at the center of his argument" (Kellerman 2012, 9). For Hobbes, the quid pro quo was simple and revealing— followers would grant absolute power to an absolute ruler who would in turn provide them with protection, first to secure their right to life and second to provide them with a life well lived.

Hobbes and Machiavelli initially seem of a piece, but Hobbes based his need for an authoritarian ruler on a different premise: the trade-off of power for protection. John Locke would expand the rights of ordinary people to include the right to liberty and the right to own property. His was the first "social contract," in which government claims derive their legitimacy from the consent of the governed. Locke insisted that unless the leader satisfied the led, he might be recalled—by force if necessary.

Leadership in the Seventeenth and Eighteenth Centuries

Clearly the period leading up to the American Revolution focused on leadership as a function of authority. Following either Hobbes or Locke, one is led to the need for authority, whether for the authority's sake or the sake of the masses. In the period that followed, the focus remained on authority, but the question for leaders became, "What makes a leader great?" For Tolstoy, given his uncommon faith in the Divine, the answer was that history is predetermined. As such, kings are slaves to history. For Carlyle, history writ large is tantamount to the history of Great Men. Considering also the writings of philosophers Herbert Spencer and William James, we can see that none of this work dealt directly with leading. These men were simply trying to answer the knottiest leadership question of the time: does the man make history, or does history make the man? It fell to philosopher John Stuart Mill to redirect scholarship to the relationship between leader and follower. This he did by expanding on the limitation of power to be suffered by the community, a limitation he calls the "very meaning of liberty."

Not unlike philosophers of his era, Mill agreed that "to prevent weaker members of a community from being preyed on by innumerable vultures, it was needful to there should be an animal of prey stronger than the rest, commissioned to keep them down" (Mill 1859). But as the king of vultures might also prey on the masses, it was necessary to defend against his intrigues. The aim of patriots, therefore, was to limit the king's power.

Mill was not just preaching against abuse of the magistrate's strength, but also against the pressure of social convention (what today we would call political correctness or PC). He believed there had to be protection from the tyranny of public opinion—possibly because he kept a lover for thirty years, marrying her only after her husband died. The romantic collaboration between Harriet Taylor and John Stuart Mill provided Mill with the inspiration to pen one of his greatest essays on liberty, *The Subjugation of Women*, called "an ardent argument for equality between the sexes, and a consequence of her influence" (Kellerman 2010, 73).

Beyond freedom from harm at the magistrate's hand, Mill believed man should be free to form his own opinions—and then to act on them without hindrance so long as the risk and peril are his own:

> Neither one person, nor any number of persons, is warranted in saying to another human of ripe years, that he shall not do with his life for his own benefit what he chooses to do with it. He is the person most interested in his own well-being: the interest which any other person, except in cases of strong personal attachment, can have in it, is trifling compared with that which he himself has. The most ordinary man or woman has means of knowledge immeasurably surpassing those that can be possessed by anyone else. (Kellerman 2010, 71).

Compare Oliver Wendell Holmes Jr.'s "My freedom to swing my arm ends with the other man's nose" (Holmes 1919).

Mill's words echo through our Declaration of Independence. Although he ignored the darker side of the human condition, Mill is on record as "the most vigorous and optimistic defender of the better angels of our nature" (Kellerman 2010, 73).

Leadership in the Nineteenth and Twentieth Centuries

Karl Marx and Friedrich Engels concerned themselves with those without power, authority, or influence. The two were concerned with the role of followership, particularly in inciting revolution. They were in the tradition of using literature as leadership rather than actually leading. Marx was a sociologist, educated in philosophy and the law; Engels was a merchant committed to overthrowing the German monarchy. The actual leader—the man who followed the blueprint of Engels and Marx—was Russia's Vladimir Lenin.

Frederick Taylor was not specifically a leader either. He was a mechanical engineer and, coincidentally, a contemporary of Lenin. He believed that workers were motivated by money. During the early days of the Industrial Revolution, he contrived the idea that piecework and strict supervision would raise performance levels. With this in mind, he invented tools to streamline production at US Steel, calculating workers' every move with the use of a stopwatch. By the 1930s, Taylor's time-and-motion studies fell out of favor (and were outlawed by Congress), but his book *The Principles of Scientific Management* (1911) was a breakthrough, lending form and substance to what leaders actually do: solve problems. Taylor's scientific steps—identify the problem, create alternate solutions, choose one, and implement—would resurface in the work of Thomas Gordon some sixty years later, but not without radical change.

Taylor was a rough-and-tumble authoritarian, sharing a dim view of human nature with Hobbes, Machiavelli, and many others who came before him. That view was about to change, with consequences for leaders everywhere.

Post–WWII Changes in the Psychology of Leading

Next in the line of leadership literature are Thomas Gordon, Douglas MacGregor, Roger Fisher, and William Ury. Yet the entire thrust of post-World War II leadership pivots around the prewar study of Abraham Maslow that led to his hierarchy of human needs.

Maslow's hierarchy is well entrenched in psychological literature, and to a sizable extent, in management. What is less known is that Maslow lived and studied on the Blackfeet Reservation during a three-month period during the 1930s for the purpose of learning how Native Americans matured into adulthood. From this experience, Maslow formulated stages of development that are pursued by individuals. He published his hierarchy in 1954, in time to profoundly influence the leadership theorists of the next sixty years.

Maslow criticized traditional psychology for its basis in study of the sick (Freud) and/or animals (B. F. Skinner). He insisted that a study of healthy people would create more and better health among individuals and society at large. His axiom—that people had a strong desire to fulfill their potential—stands as a paradigm shift in the way we look at men and women in the workplace. His is the seminal development in the study of leadership that influenced scholarship (and management) up to and including the present.

Maslow's hierarchy states that humans are motivated by the pursuit of unmet needs. According to this theory, if fundamental needs are not satisfied, humans will be motivated to satisfy those. Higher needs, such as those for socialization and esteem, are not recognized until the basic needs of existence—air, water, food, safety—are satisfied. Such pursuit is not linear; individuals move up and down the needs hierarchy and even reach for multiple successes at the same time. Yet Maslow's model is useful for charting advancement in social cultures as well as in mapping individual attainment.

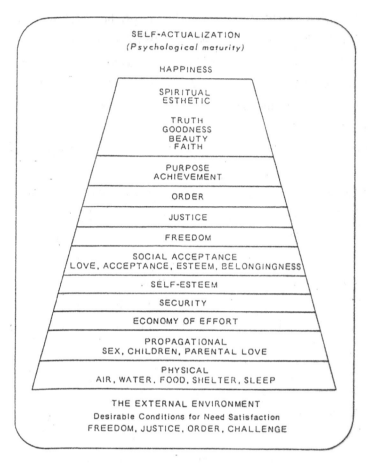

Source: Maurice Bassett, Publisher

My intent here is not to dissect Maslow's pioneering work so much as to pinpoint its seldom-noted uniqueness. For the most part, in Western circles—North American culture in particular—basic human needs are satisfied. What is intriguing is Maslow's Meta or growth needs, in which social and esteem needs become the primary goal. Note how our schools have prepared young people to achieve these needs. Meta needs like friendship, belonging to a group, giving and receiving love, and eventually recognition, attention, social status, accomplishment, and self-respect are the preeminent needs of our entire society. They are especially keen among the young. Thanks to teachers, these needs are honored in the classroom, even if misunderstood and underappreciated by education's critics.

An early disciple of Maslow, and the man who gets credit for spoiling the Hobbesian view of human nature, was Douglas MacGregor. MacGregor was in fact a contemporary of Maslow who conceived the notion that people were not adverse to work—disputing the old Theory X, which says that most people find work innately distasteful and will attempt to avoid it. MacGregor countered with Theory Y, that work can be as natural as play if the conditions are favorable. In *The Human Side of Enterprise* (1960), MacGregor noted that people will be self-directed to meet work objectives and committed to quality and productivity, but only if rewards are in place that address higher needs. Moreover, most people can handle responsibility because creativity and ingenuity are common in the population.

MacGregor makes the point that a command-and-control environment is not effective because it relies on lower needs for motivation. In Western society, lower needs are mostly satisfied and thus no longer motivate. In a top-down environment, one would expect employees to dislike their work, to avoid responsibility, to have no interest in organizational goals, and to resist change, thus creating a self-fulfilling prophecy. To MacGregor, healthy motivation seemed more likely with his Theory Y model (MacGregor 2015, para. 4).

Next in line are the men who leveraged Maslow's hierarchy to create leader models of their own: Thomas Gordon, Roger Fisher, and William Ury. As we will see in the next chapter on basic collaboration, Gordon redefined interpersonal problems so that they reflected the underlying needs of contrary positions. For example, in a teacher–student conflict, the parties might put their heads together in a search for solutions that might work, and then decide which solution would be best for meeting the needs of both teacher and student. Gordon's book *Teacher Effectiveness Training* (1974) sold in the millions, as did his *Leader Effectiveness Training* (1977). More about Tom Gordon in chapters 2 and 4.

Fisher and Ury, authors of *Getting to Yes: Negotiating Agreement Without Giving In* (1981) and cofounders of the Harvard Negotiation Project, differ from Tom Gordon in that they prefer the term "underlying interests" to Gordon's "underlying needs"—understandable since their project is aimed at corporate America. Where Gordon's efforts targeted interpersonal problems that stifle teamwork and creativity in schools, Fisher and Ury's canvas is the corporate workplace. For example, negotiations between Simpson Lumber Company and the federal government about the spotted owl in the 1980s revealed the following interests: Simpson needed a promise of long-range sustainability and the feds needed protection for the endangered species. Together the sides produced the well-known solution that created islands of tree stands as a home for the birds. The government found the process so inviting that it offered Simpson a ten-year moratorium on federal oversight of the company's forests.

In another convincing example, Alaskan fishermen had for decades been herded by the federal fisheries department into fishing on designated days, similar to hunters who find their prey only in season. The halibut fishermen were intensely troubled because when their season arrived, they were forced to ply the waters without benefit of reliable weather. On average, five fishermen or women were drowned each year when Derby Day was in effect.

Working with their halibut men, the Alaskan authorities solved the problem by limiting the season to a given number of days, yet allowing boats to go out at the discretion of the crew. The total purse was now shared by the boats on a prorated basis. The new schedule protected the halibut species while preserving human life. The resulting regulation created high morale among the fleet and made millionaires out of many of its crew.

Together with Tom Gordon, Fisher and Ury are responsible for much that transpired in leadership circles during the 1990s. During that decade, the *transactional* leadership of Machiavelli, Hobbes, and others was replaced by *transformational* leadership, designed to unite leader and follower through the use of decentralized decision making. Transactional leaders—like Harry "the buck stops here" Truman or George "I am the decider" Bush—pronounce decisions. In contrast, transformational leaders deliberate with their workers so as to stimulate a mutual goal orientation within their team. Where transactional leaders believe optimal solutions stem from conflicting positions, the much preferred transformational leader believes peak solutions originate through a blending of diverse intentions and ideas. An abbreviated form of transformational leadership is the school mission statement, a product of the 1990s.

Next in Line: Servant Leadership

Next in leadership's lineage is the servant leadership of Robert Greenleaf. Writing as a contemporary of Thomas Gordon, Greenleaf opined:

> Servant-leaders focus primarily on the growth and well-being of people and the communities to which they belong. While traditional leadership generally involves the accumulation and exercise of power by one at the top of the hierarchy, servant leadership upends the pyramid. The servant-leader yields power, puts the needs of others first and helps people develop and perform as highly as possible. (Greenleaf 2015, para. 5)

Well-known leadership theorists like Ken Blanchard, Stephen Covey, and Margaret Wheatley are among those who subscribe to servant leadership.

Greenleaf turns the traditional leadership hierarchy on its head; his theory is idealistic on its own and a hard concept to visualize in practice. Nevertheless, in short form, we can say that the transactional leader controls power, the transformational leader shares power, and the servant leader shuns power altogether. Greenleaf assumes employees whose needs are addressed will graciously labor for their employer's needs at the same time. Unlike Greenleaf, Gordon believes needs are better aired, balanced, and satisfied through a collaborative process. Collaborative leading is where we turn next.

CHAPTER

2

BASIC COLLABORATION

Where in the world is someone who can
teach our children how to collaborate?
—Hank Rubin

Remember the age of empowerment? Of decentralized decision making? Of the flattened hierarchy? The 1990s were billed as the time when teachers were granted access to school decision making. By the turn of the century, group meetings—often poorly timed and crudely organized—faced a backlash that resulted in the dismantling of shared decision making and the restoring of command and control. As *Kappan Magazine* noted in 2010:

> Teacher collaboration is a prime determinant of school improvement. Unfortunately, though we talk about it a lot, we don't do it as much as we might hope for. We take pride when we see a few random acts of collaboration in our schools, but the *modal* behavior in schools has changed little over the years ... even in schools that claim to have professional learning communities. (Piercey, 55)

As readers might imagine, participatory leadership in the twenty-first century will operate from a structured framework, unlike the amorphous meetings of the 1990s. Similarly, collaborating will mean more than partnering. Anyone can lead a collaborative, but to lead collaboratively? That is a different process indeed. And what about students? Classroom leading too can be collaborative. Why are students not included when teachers render their decisions?

Collaborative leadership, first envisioned for the classroom by Thomas Gordon during the second half of the twentieth century, designates a problem-solving sequence. The six-step arc closely resembles Frederick Taylor's scientific steps, but by focusing on human needs, Gordon removes power from the leader and involves followers equally with superiors when deciding. Gordon redefines problems in such a way that human needs are acknowledged, and in fact, achieved. It is truly a no-lose proposition, and that is the moniker it gained when Gordon promoted it in *Teacher Effectiveness Training*: the No-Lose Method of Leadership (1974, 217). Thomas Gordon and the men who influenced him are where we turn next.

The Gordon Innovation

Gordon, a much-admired bomber pilot over Germany during World War II, was disabused of his traditional leadership notions in the years following the end of the war. His commitment to look after the welfare of his airmen did not transfer well to the civilian environment. To resolve this painful enigma, Gordon earned his doctorate in psychology in the 1950s. In the process, he became enamored with Maslow's hierarchy. Could this be the piece he was missing?

It occurred to Gordon that student needs were often obscured by a teacher's fascination with control. Still, such needs appeared valid, and if expressed openly could be accepted by the teacher. The trick would be to get teacher and student to reveal their needs, and here the gentle prodding of the psychologist in Gordon shone through.

At the University of Chicago, Gordon wrote his dissertation on including followers' needs when making decisions, calling it Method Three or No-Lose Leadership. His work was roundly dismissed. Rather than give up, Gordon published his dissertation, *Teacher Effectiveness Training*, independently. It became an instant hit and remained on the *New York Times* best-seller list for more than thirty months.

I met Dr. Gordon through my reading and through his Effectiveness Institute in Solana Beach, California. For his efforts at redefining workplace, classroom, and family problems, he received three nominations for the Nobel Peace Prize. His dream of obtaining a Nobel was never realized, and he passed away in 2002.

Gordon believed the presenting problem—the adversarial dilemma as viewed by opposing parties—was seldom the actual problem. The real problem lay hidden among human needs. The conundrum for leaders was to identify those needs and set them in balance. Gordon wrote that leaders would be more effective if they asked, "How can we meet the needs of student A at the same time we meet the needs of teacher B?"

For example: Teacher Leanne Aten was having trouble keeping the halls quiet when her fifth graders returned from recess. When she collaborated with her class, she learned that her students needed a few minutes to talk. Leanne's need was not to disturb the other classrooms. When she asked, "How can we have both?" her problem disappeared in a slew of ideas from her kids. "Now I allow them a little time to visit when returning to the room. The conflict no longer exists! My students are quiet in the halls, and they have a few minutes to chat" (personal communication/written assignment, 1998).

This is the Gordon method at work. But because it involves a concrete sequence and not just a single innovation, it invites a closer look. Before we take that, I want to mention two moments between Gordon's steps when collaborations come to grief. One is what I call the *setup*, and the other I call the *cross-check*. The setup is where the leader gains permission to influence a new and different process. It is designed to gently shut the door on stakeholders bowing out before the collaboration is complete. Here is Leanne, setting the stage:

> I explained to my class that we have a problem and that I would like to solve it in a way that we would all feel good. I asked the class if this was a good time, and if anyone felt it was not enough time we could reschedule. No one raised their hand. I explained that I had taken a class designed to help solve situations where both sides are happy with the outcome. I asked permission to use this strategy and everybody agreed.

The importance of the setup cannot be overstated. Without it, the path is open to anyone who wants to defect or wants to sabotage the process because of some unstated need. The preamble goes like this:

- Introduce yourself as a facilitator rather than the decider.
- State the purpose (so both sides win).
- Ask if the time is good.
- Ask if it is enough time.
- Ask if the students are willing to try something new.
- Begin assessing needs.

Each item in this sequence is crucial. Teachers might not have control of the outcome, but they do have control of the process. Such modest control is asserted right from the start. Teachers should feel the leader's reins in their hands.

For the cross-check, the problem-solving sequence is placed on pause while the facilitator confirms that the stakeholders still understand and are committed to the process. I will discuss the cross-check in detail in the next section.

Gordon's Six-Step Model

Once the setup is complete, students are ready to collaborate. Following a brief outline, we will delve into each of the steps in detail. The steps in order are as follows:

1. Define the problem as balancing the needs of both sides.
2. Brainstorm for solutions.
3. Evaluate ideas.
4. Choose the solution.
5. Implement the solution.
6. Follow up on progress.

The cross-check comes between steps one and two. The descriptions that follow assume that collaboration is best learned from the position of third-party facilitator. In the above example, Aten acted as both stakeholder and facilitator, normally a perilous way to learn.

Step 1: Defining Problems in Terms of Needs

After a successful setup, moving directly to needs is advisable. Listing needs as they are expressed is helpful to stakeholders, as they can then track the Gordon sequence. A whiteboard or legal pad may be employed. Experienced facilitators know that listing needs in a nonjudgmental fashion will allow deeper needs to flow to the surface.

Once listed, needs will invariably lend themselves to an umbrella word or phrase—a condensation of several needs into one summarizing desire (see appendix 1). Then an equation can be drawn so that the stakeholders can readily track the process. On the board, the facilitator might write: *How can we meet the needs of the teacher (A) while also meeting the needs of the students (B)?* Moving forward is simply a case of plugging in the underlying needs. For example, on the subject of wearing hats in the classroom, the equation will look like: *How can we have students express their individuality while we maintain order in the room?* This becomes a problem with many viable solutions.

Please note that for this chapter, the concern is not with secret needs or angry rebuttals. Chapter 3 studies such advanced cases. The object at this time is to learn the Gordon steps, and to do so as a neutral facilitator. Also, in order to focus on learning the steps, full and honest disclosure of the stakeholders is expected—at least hoped for.

The Cross-Check: Transitioning Step 1 to Step 2

Before examining solutions, check to make sure that both sides are invested in the process. In a real-time collaboration, if a cross-check is not completed, one or both parties might revert back to blaming the other for the problem. Blame is the last thing you want. Collaboration must be a blame-free method.

Check with stakeholders individually to see if they want to change their side of the equation. If not, feel free to move ahead. Make sure each side understands the needs of the other. To complete the cross-check, ask the tell-all question: *Is it okay for the other party to have the need(s) expressed?* Failure to complete the cross-check means the collaboration is at risk. Other than Gordon's redefining the problem, the cross-check is the most vital part of the process and the reason, if any, for a collaborative endeavor falling apart.

Step 2: Searching for Solutions

Once the crosscheck is complete, the facilitator can relax to an extent. Ideally, he or she can invite silly and even untenable solutions. Laughter opens the mind to new ideas. Apart from the newness of the steps, this should be a stress-free time. Both sides are comfortable with the process, and the facilitator has kept them from opening a figurative door and fleeing. Each party has had the opportunity to disclose individual needs and honor the other person's needs. By following the guidelines of brainstorming, they search for solutions together. When one party offers a solution that mainly meets the other person's need, the second person will often offer an idea that reciprocates. That is when the job of the facilitator is significantly, although not completely, done.

Step 3: Evaluating Solutions

A successful collaboration should begin to crystallize a solution. Often in the interest of time, Step 4—choosing solutions—can immediately follow Step 2. If you find it necessary to evaluate ideas one at a time, try using the T model that Benjamin Franklin introduced to chart financial accounts. This method takes longer, but because of its thoroughness, I prefer it in sticky situations.

To set up a T chart, create two columns and head the left side with a minus sign and the right side with a plus. Now list limitations on the left and advantages on the right. Do this for each possible solution. When completed, a page full of T charts (and evaluations for each one) should result. You might have four advantages on the plus side and only one limitation, yet that one disadvantage is a genuine liability to one party. You'll need to calibrate that in your outcome rather than simply count pros and cons. This method isolates, or flags, bad ideas. It also demonstrates that your stakeholders are working together to solve their problem.

Step 4: Choosing Solutions

By this time in a collaboration, a truly satisfying solution will have bubbled to the surface. Often a number of ideas are acceptable to the stakeholders. Those can be combined. Within reason, several courses of action may be worth pursuing at the same time.

Step 5: Implementing Solutions

Not much needs to be said here except that people who solve problems together implement solutions together. That axiom applies to any group process. It simply reflects the truism that students will be more eager to do what *they* decide to do than what others decide for them.

Teacher Art Sabiston found problems when his shop class regularly failed to clean up properly. After his collaboration ended, he wrote to me saying, "The boys are cleaning without problems since they claimed ownership of the collaboration and accepted responsibility for cleaning relevant areas of the shop" (personal communication 2013).

Step 6: Course Corrections/Following Up

A good idea from the start is to monitor progress as the stakeholders move forward with their solution. This can be on a daily or weekly basis, or it can mean simply reconvening at a later date. At that time, the team can modify its solution, pick another solution, or set a time for further evaluation of what's being done. More will be said about follow-up in chapter 3.

Historic Roots of Collaboration: The Crow Ritual

Native Americans lived in closer proximity to one another than we do in modern America. Tribes could be presumed to have councils and other means of settling matters in dispute. Some even had elaborate rituals to celebrate peaceful methods. I learned the following example from workshop leaders at the Association of Experiential Education. Stemming from the Crow nation, it lends a kinetic element to my own workshops and can be acted out at home or in the classroom. When enacted in the classroom, the ritual seems to find a comfortable spot in children's memories.

The Crow rite of passage was used to initiate young people into tribal membership. With the preteens waiting outside the tent or building, an elder would call one child into the tribe. There the juvenile would be told to face a second elder and join hands with this elder. Once they had joined hands at shoulder height, the two would be asked to push and shove without result. The presiding elder would ask the child, "Is that the way you want to solve problems with your brother?" Dutifully, the youngster would reply, "No."

The two would repeat the effort, but this time the elder would tumble, reeling across the room. "Is that the way you want to solve problems?" "No."

Finally, when the youngster shoved a third time, the elder would loop one hand overhead so that their hands, still clenched, were side by side. "Now where is your problem?" the youngster was asked. Out in front was the answer. "Where is your vision?" Focused on the problem. "How are you standing?" Side by side. "Where are your shoulders?" Touching, joined. The elder and the boy were shoulder-to-shoulder facing the symbol of their problem. A second child joined with the initial juvenile, and the process was repeated, and so forth.

It is unfortunate that it's necessary to go back thousands of years to find a metaphor for collaborating, but there it is. Teachers can take this ritual back to their classrooms both as a look at Native American folklore and as a beginning for understanding collaboration.

Facilitating a Six-Step Process

To repeat, the Gordon method is best learned as a neutral facilitator. This provides an opportunity to become comfortable with the steps without having to protect a need of your own. Facilitating without a neutral third party is a difficult and often misunderstood process. A closer look at two-party collaboration will be found in chapter 3. For now, three-party facilitation is the rule—the facilitator and two others we will call stakeholders, or simply parties committed to solving a problem.

First, the facilitator introduces the process. This is the setup mentioned above. State the purpose (so that both will win), confirm the time frame in two parts (is it a good time and enough time), and ask if the parties are willing to try something new.

Once permission to influence is achieved, go directly to needs. Start with the person who brought up the problem. This is simply a good-will gesture allowing that person to feel his or her appeal is getting the attention it deserves.

When assessing needs, pay particular attention to notions the other party is likely to respect. Remember—the cross-check is within reach to get the parties side by side. But for now, only list the needs. You will want firm control of your process, and that is gained by guiding each step in sequence without letting one party or the other get ahead. The rule of thumb is this: It is okay to go backward in the steps but it is not okay to get ahead. This allows participants to modify their needs as they witness the collaborative effort helping out. It also lets the parties add solutions when they come to mind after Step 2 is complete.

If one party gets ahead of the process, it is best to gently deflect the comment. When one person, say, offers a solution while I am still assessing needs, I say, "I know you'd like to see that solution. Remind me when we get to Step 2. I will begin with your idea." This gentle handling of the disruption allows the facilitator to remain an effective listener while bringing the Gordon sequence back online.

When assessing needs, pay particular attention to what I call "umbrella" statements—summaries that seem to encompass several spoken needs. For example, in a bullying situation, "You need to feel safe" will normally cover several needs: the need to not be hit, not be teased, not be threatened, etc. Umbrella phrases also fill in one side of the collaboration equation in a manner that is hard to rebut. The bully has to understand his victim's need to feel safe or he will oust himself from the process.

Mutual understanding is completed with the cross-check, which is that important transition between Steps 1 and 2. Only when the cross-check is complete and there is full acceptance of everybody's needs does solution-finding come into play. Here the guidelines of brainstorming apply. At all costs, resist giving solutions. At this stage, the worst mistake facilitators can make is to give the best solution. Solving stakeholders' problems for them undermines ownership. It deflates the process in one innocent move.

As a third-party facilitator, you will need to record key pieces of information: individual needs, summary words (or phrases), collaboration equations, solutions, evaluations, and assignments. The process ends when stakeholders agree on their assignment—or agree to continue the discussion at a later time. Here is the completed process as submitted by a master's level student. The written assignment is provided here as reported by teacher Debbi Wallace. Her report is quoted verbatim. (Where the need is for emphasis, the italics are mine.)

> **The Problem:** This collaboration takes place between Monica and David, ten-year-olds in my fourth grade classroom. They had been matched as partners for a cooperative learning activity. They were to choose a topic from the information on insects we'd been studying and present it to the class. They had been at a stalemate all morning as to how to present information on their chosen topic, "How Crickets Sing." They had asked for my help. I gave encouragement and suggested that they listen to each other's wishes. By 10 a.m., they were not talking at all.
>
> I perceived what I thought was their problem. Instead of telling them this time, I decided it would be a great time to use my collaborator skills to help

25

them discover each other's needs. The following is an overview of what took place.

The Setup: I set things up informally as both agreed to use their library time to try this new process. They were anxious, but willing. We began with Monica stating her needs.

Trolling for Needs: Monica needed to get the work done, to have it look good, not to have to do all the work, and to have fun.

David's needs were much slower in coming and difficult for him to state. David needed to get it done, not get in trouble, and not miss recess and to have help. At this point, I repeated David's last comment to him. He said, "Yes, it's too hard." Monica reminded David that he had agreed to the topic of crickets. "I know, but I don't want to write it." I wrote that on his list: David doesn't want to write.

David added, "I can't read that stuff." I asked if he needed help in reading and he said he did. I wrote "help with reading." By now, Monica's face was wide-eyed with surprise and David was shifting in his chair.

I introduced the needs equation. I reminded them that they would both be winners when we were done. Monica's side was easy for her to see. I led David through a slow questioning process (which Monica listened to intently) and in the end he stated his own need. The equation looked like this: *How could we finish the project so that Monica doesn't have all the work and David gets help and feels smart?*

I checked with them so they understood and accepted each other's need. Monica, especially, was very enthusiastic and supportive. "I didn't know what you needed!" she grinned.

Possible Solutions: From here on things went quickly. They easily created a list of solutions, rejected a few, and came up with a plan. I spoke only a word or two and they did the rest.

1. Get an adult to help.
2. Use drawings/diagrams.
3. Monica writes and David draws.
4. Do a game show.
5. Monica reads and David picks important stuff to do (act out).
6. Make a video.
7. Write a story about a cricket.
8. Read together.

Evaluating Solutions: [Author's note: The Wallace report is shown verbatim. Unlike the T chart, the children apparently evaluated their solutions by quickly throwing out those less tenable and combining the remaining four.]

Choosing the Solution: Monica put their basic ideas into a (combined) plan involving solutions two, three, five, and eight. They could draw pictures showing the information and write a sentence with each one, explaining what it means. David added that he could act it out. "It would be funny," he said with a grin.

I had them tell me what they thought they should do now. They decided to read the book at the same time and Monica would write down the needed sentences. David would draw diagrams to go with the sentences and they would color them together. David also agreed to act out the part of a "singing" cricket, much to Monica's relief! They both agreed to this solution and said they felt much better.

Implementing the Solution: That afternoon, they were talking and listening to each other. Monica was eager to help David. He even had to back her off a bit. She asked for his opinion and he offered to help in many ways. Smiles were plentiful.

A postscript from Debbi Wallace: "David has a learning disability and reads at a low first-grade level. David is learning to express his needs and to work through his difficulties, not ignore them. This was a giant step for him. Monica, obviously, had no idea about David's weakness in reading. She is bright and sometimes quiet in new situations. If I had told them what they should do, David wouldn't have communicated his needs and Monica would have missed out on the chance to truly understand."

One Note of Caution

The job of a third-party facilitator like Debbi is to do more than guide the steps. She has to take care to keep aggressive remarks out of the needs assessment and translate any need that suggests a change in the other stakeholder's behavior. So for *Monica needs David to help more,* Debbi would have written *Monica not have to do all the work.* Remember—it is Monica whose needs are being assessed. Likewise, for David's need for *Monica to help with reading,* Debbi would note *for David to get help with reading.* Using the passive voice to remain neutral is key to success.

During the needs assessment, particularly in an adversarial or competitive situation, the person who feels aggrieved will often demand the other party do (or stop doing) a certain behavior. If this is not redirected, it can lead back to bickering and reignite the disagreement. It takes experience to catch these traps and disable them, but it is not hard to do. Simply keep names out of the picture by changing to the passive voice.

When a facilitator hears, "To get Frankie to stop hitting me," he or she repeats, "For you to not be hit." This will almost certainly lead to the deeper need, "To feel safe at school," and presto—you have a need a bully can sign off on, or lose his best chance to escape harsher resolution. The idea is to get a needs equation that both parties can accept. The best way to do that is to quietly remove names from the needs assessment.

Summary

Any negotiation that seeks to balance underlying needs is a collaboration. Any discussion based on superficial desires is a partnership, not a collaboration. When learning to collaborate, look for an issue that can be resolved by a neutral third party and one where full disclosure is expected. This keeps beginners focused on the process and not on the behavior of the participants. Make sure to complete the critical junctures cleanly and clearly, and try not to proceed without those. These are the setup and the cross-check. In both cases, one's instincts will tell whether the stakeholders are invested and ready to move forward.

With that in mind, return to Gordon's six-step method. Go through the steps one at a time, allowing the parties to go back to an earlier step but not forward, getting ahead of the process. Control the collaboration; do not control the people. For example, say, "Thanks. We will evaluate solutions when we get more ideas on the board. Meantime, hold that thought. We'll need it when we measure solutions."

Translate aggressive comments so that they become innocuous to the other party. Simply change to the passive voice. This is best done by keeping names out of the assessment. Get closure to each process or be exact about when it will continue. Get commitment to the solution from all stakeholders along with roles to be played when implementing the new idea.

Teachers are changing the power balance in their classrooms. They are demonstrating the truth of "to surrender power is to gain power." They are finding children eager for collaborating to work, excited about one another, and thrilled with the results.

ADVANCED COLLABORATION

First pants then your shoes.
—Gary Larson, *The Far Side*

If you think collaboration's six-step process looks like conflict resolution, you would be correct. However, many who study conflict are humbled and dismayed to learn how hard it is to deal with, especially when they, as stakeholders, are part of the dispute. For the most part, conflict-resolution workshops demonstrate that resolution is *possible*; however, the art and science of conflict resolution is something left to the experts. Unless, of course, it is taught as a special case of collaboration, and then it is simply an aftermarket bolt-on to the basic design.

Imagine a stream running along a map until it reaches a bridge. But the bridge, symbolizing conflict, is destroyed, and it has fallen into the water to block traffic. Upstream of that damage lies conflict resolution. Upstream of that lies conflict prevention, and still farther upstream problem solving. Farther upstream of problem solving is problem prevention, and farther than that, routine decision making.

The purpose of chapter 2 was not only to introduce problem solving using the collaborative model but also to enable teachers and staff to adopt a vocabulary that keeps the focus on human needs. As such, it provides a structure for ordinary deciding. Safety of individual staff members, particularly emotional safety, depends on this type of teaming in the school. Fundamental to the desired context is bargaining over the shared problem and never over entrenched positions (Fisher and Ury 1981, 38).

With this in mind, we will examine what happens to the collaborative moment when parties will not reveal their needs. Other advanced scenarios occur when the collaborating parties are hostile, when there is both anger and hidden agenda, when there are multiple parties to the negotiations, and when there is no neutral person to mediate (a particularly difficult situation). Here, the skilled party must protect his or her needs while also facilitating the event. The schematic shown below illustrates how incremental training proceeds.

Collaborating with Hidden Needs

Throughout chapter 2, we assumed full disclosure on the part of A and B. More than that, we assumed that novice facilitators will first attempt the Gordon process as neutral parties. This allows them to be uninterested in outcomes and able to focus on the problem-solving sequence. The next development would be facilitating when the parties do not reveal their needs. This is represented by the dotted line connecting parties A and B in the schematic below.

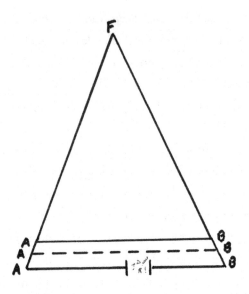

SIDEBAR

The diagram above shows the training model used in my workshops as well as in this book. Training in collaboration is designed to be incremental, developmental so that information builds on that which is already learned.

Here, A and B are parties to the collaboration represented by the straight line at the bottom of the triangle (full disclosure). The (neutral) facilitator is designated F. The dashed line represents parties holding a hidden agenda and the 'blocked' and final line indicates lack of communication and often conflict.

When collaborating amid hidden needs, the facilitator must dredge up those needs so that they can be winnowed down to the collaborative equation. Recall from the previous chapter that needs start out as basic to human existence and then become more sublime as one progresses through life. Unmet needs dictate where parties A and B are entering the process. The way to bring them into play is to listen.

Active listening means hearing what is said and communicating to participants that they are being attended to—in other words, heard. Schoolteachers, thanks to decades of emphasis, are perfectly adept at active listening. They practice it every day. They teach children how to listen, although perhaps not as directly as in the Gordon method. Their teaching is by example. Listening engenders trust in the process, which is equally important to helping uncover hidden needs. Listen effectively, and you will get the buy-in from participants you require.

I am indebted to consultant David Landsburg of Tucson, Arizona, for his *Non-Directive Listening for Managers*, the most succinct introduction to attending skills I am aware of. Below is the Landsburg handout, inserted here with permission.

O-COMM CONCEPTS

Non-Directive Listening for Managers

Research studies suggest that the number one subordinate complaint about managers is that they do not listen. Part of the reason for those findings is that, indeed, managers may not listen enough. Another part of the reason is that managers may not give enough feedback to their employees indicating that they are trying to listen.

Carl Rogers developed a counseling technique which is called either "Active Listening" or "Non-directive listening." It is based on the concept that a counselor or psychologist can help a client solve his problem by listening to him in a non-directive manner. This same approach can be used by managers to help employees solve their own problems. Such a practice encourages personal growth on the part of employees. It also means that employees are more apt to buy into the solution, since they developed it themselves.

Rules

The following list of six rules gives a basic overview of the non-directive listening process.

1. **Take time** to listen carefully. Non-directive listening cannot be hurried. If you have an important appointment in a few minutes, do not start non-directive listening. Instead, set an appointment to deal with the problem at a later time.

2. **Be attentive** to the employee. Concentrate your total attention on what the employee is saying.

3. **Give three verbal reactions.** Those reactions are all designed to show the employee that you are trying to understand what is being said. Yet, you do not want to direct the conversation. The reactions are silence (the employee will usually fill the silence by telling you more), intelligent grunts (such as "uh huh") which say I understand, but still do not direct the conversation, and paraphrasing, which involves repeating what you heard in terms of both content and feelings.

4. **Use no aggressive probes.** Your natural curiosity will often cause you to want to ask specific questions to get more information. However, that makes you the director and reduces the probability that the employee will solve the problem himself.

5. **Never evaluate** what the employee is telling you. You do not disagree with him. Nor, do you say you support his opinion. Employees will often want your opinion. However, if you give

them an opinion, you begin to direct them in the problem solving process. This may not be in their best interest.

6. **Never lose faith** in the ability of the employee to solve the problem. The principle on which this system works is that people can solve their own problems. By solving the problem herself, the employee becomes more committed to making the solution work, and at the same time develops problem solving skills.

The underlying principle is that the manager should give lots of feedback which says to the employee that "I really want to understand what you are saying."

<u>When to Use</u>

Using this technique will get you high marks from employees who want their managers to listen to them more. It might also improve employee commitment to the task. However, the total technique cannot be used in all situations. Consider the following four factors when deciding whether or not to use non-directive listening in any specific situation.

1. Confirm that you are discussing a **complex problem**. It is probably not worth getting into the process if the employee just wants to know whether to use form A or form B.

2. Make certain you have the **necessary time and commitment** to go through the process. It is not wise to start the non-directive listening process, only to cut the conversation short to move on to a more important matter.

3. Be sure that you can **withhold judgement** on the issue. It is admirable to help employees in solving problems. However, you must be able to live with whatever solution is selected. If the employee is trying to decide whether or not it is appropriate to drink alcohol at lunch time, there may be company policy which already makes the decision.

4. Only use the process **in proportion**. Employees will grow very tired of intelligent grunts and nodding silence if you use the technique all the time.

Americans are feeling increasingly alienated -- from neighbors, from families, from companies. People are looking for someone who will listen to them -- someone to whom they can be committed. By using some portion or all of the process of non-directive listening, you can help employees solve their own problems, increase their commitment to the company and increase their commitment to you as a manager.

Incidentally, the same principles work for salespeople, especially during the interview phase when you are trying to discover the customer's felt needs.

DAVID L. LANDSBURG

9160 E. Holmes • Tucson, Arizona 85710   (602) 885-1602

One technique missing from Landsburg's approach is a device for encouraging participants to open up—the upward inflection of a spoken word indicating that one is asking a question. Pay attention and you will hear this in everyday conversation. Effective facilitators will choose a keyword or phrase and simply repeat it using an upward tilt. For example, one party might say, "I didn't know it was that far away."

Try saying, "That far away?"

"Yes, because it will take me longer to get there."

"Take longer?"

"I can't get away early. I'm afraid I'll walk in late." And so on.

People enjoy being attended to. This simple maneuver helps them get in touch with hidden needs and articulate them to the facilitator. It also builds trust, both in the facilitator and in the process. Of course, one might say, "Tell me more about that …" or "Say more on that …" Still, as indicated by Landsburg's title, active listening tends to be nondirective.

On the other hand, a steady diet of listening can irritate. So be ready to alternate this with a direct approach. Just know that you are there to build trust. Your purpose from the beginning is to see that both sides of the collaboration win.

An Example of Facilitating with Unspoken Needs

A local Kiwanis club was weeks away from installing new officers. The outgoing and incoming presidents were caucusing to develop fresh ideas. The new president—I'll call him Allan—suggested changing the first meeting of the month to a general meeting rather than a director's meeting, as had been the long-standing tradition. This meant coming up with a schedule for board meetings outside the accepted monthly practice, as well as having a fifth meeting each month.

The outgoing president—I'll call him Jim—immediately said, "I can tell you, I'd be against a change like that."

"Why?" Allan asked. "I want to give that monthly meeting back to the general membership."

"I'm just against it," Jim said. "I see no reason for the change."

After a few minutes of this, I asked, "Would you guys mind if I facilitated here?" I went through the checklist for opening a collaboration, ending with my purpose to see that both men were taken care of. They agreed. Our dialogue continued as follows:

Me: Allan, what are your needs around shifting that first meeting over to the members?

Allan: Meetings are fun. I want to share them with the rest, like every week.

Me: What does it do for you to extend that initial meeting to everybody?

Allan: I don't know.

Me: What would it be if you did know? (Another gambit on my part)

Allan: I'm not sure. (Gambit failed)

Me: Jim, what do you need around these meetings?

Jim: I need things to stay the way they are.

Me: You're content with the status quo.

Jim: Well, sure. I can't come to a separate board meeting no matter when.

Me: Can't come?

Jim: I travel farthest anyway. I just can't add one more meeting.

Me: So it's economical—just travel to three meetings a month plus one board meeting.

Jim: Yes.

Me: Let's enter that in the equation—Jim needs to economize his travels. Allan, have you identified your need around changing it up?

Allan: I think I would like to identify myself as caring about the membership, about making a decision that favors their interests.

Me: We can enter that. But it seems as if we have a third party to these negotiations. How do we know what members want?

Jim: I don't know of any dissatisfaction with the way things are. Why not see what the members want?

At this point, we agreed to this collaboration equation: *How can we meet Jim's need for economizing his travel so that we meet Allan's need for acting in favor of the group?* Next on our agenda would be to raise the question in front of the membership. In fact, private conversations showed that no one actually wanted four open meetings per month. The issue was dropped, saving Allan from raising a question he could not pursue.

Collaborating with Angry People

Given the way Allan and Jim started out, I feel sure things would have become heated without our dialog. Jim had already dug in his heels, and Allan had frustrated both Jim and I by not being able to identify his need. But what do facilitators do when issues begin to go up in flames?

Let's go back to the beginning for a moment. In your setup, you will need to add a key ingredient if anger is present (or anticipated). This is the one rule that governs collaboration: *only one person can talk at a time.* I call this the Angry Rule, and my suggestion is not to invoke it unless aggressive feelings are on the horizon. My reasoning is that people are hounded by enough rules, and they can only open up if they are free of restrictions, even if just for the moment. Once again, the Angry Rule is part of the setup, and it only needs to be mentioned if anger is present. Facilitating amid anger is symbolized by the communication blockage between A and B in the collaboration diagram. F continues as the neutral facilitator.

By this time in the incremental sequence, we are at conflict resolution, but we have arrived by a very different route. By treating conflict resolution as a special case of collaboration, we can assume there is an overlay of skilled communication in place in your classroom or school building. This makes resolving conflict easy, for the following reasons:

1. Followers are comfortable with the collaborative overlay and eager to get back to it.

2. Despite the urban myth that people love to fight, they actually like resolution.

3. Angry people will tell you what they need.

You will simply need a recipe for turning the anger around so that it works in your favor. Before you do that, you can profit from what all professional counselors have carved on their desks: "Hear the feelings first!"

An Example of Facilitating Amid Anger

Teacher and volleyball coach Steven Johnson describes what happened when conflict erupted between two girls, affecting the performance of his team:

> Nikki and Tonya are friends normally, having played together for the past three years. When catty remarks occurred in the past, and with time at a premium, I would attempt to solve the problem using an authoritarian approach: "All right, ladies, what's the problem? Here is the solution, now get back to practice."
>
> Thirty minutes into practice, Nikki said, "You could have gotten that ball if you would just more your feet."
>
> **Introduction:** I called Tonya and Nikki over and expressed that I was concerned about the friction that was developing between them and that I wanted to help them both have their needs met. When I asked if it was a good time, both girls said no; they wanted to keep on with practice but could stay after to resolve the issue.
>
> After practice, I repeated my concern and asked if they were willing to try a new process that will allow them both to get their needs met. Both agreed. I then told them that in order for the process to work, only one person could talk at a time. Again, they both agreed.

Steven: Tonya, let's begin with you. What are your needs?

Tonya: (animated) I need the coach to provide feedback, not Nikki.

Steven: You feel strongly that I'm the one to give criticism.

Tonya: Yes. And I need Nikki to treat me with respect.

Nikki: (talking over) But how can I respect you if you don't support me in the games?

Steven: (hand up to Nikki) Nikki, remember. We'll get to your needs in a moment.

Nikki: (nods)

Steven: (to Tonya) It's respect then, isn't it? You need to be respected on the floor.

Tonya: Not just in volleyball, all the time.

Steven: I understand.

I then asked Nikki to assess her needs.

Nikki: I need Tonya to support me in games and in practice.

Steven: You need to be supported.

Nikki: Yes, and I need Tonya to give me a chance to give input when the team is in a huddle.

Steven: Input in the huddle?

Nikki: Yes. You know, when we huddle up. That's when Tonya cuts me off. She has a bad habit.

Steven: So it happens regularly. And that makes you mad.

Nikki: Well, sure.

Steven: Do I understand, Nikki, that you need support from the team and to give input in the huddle?

Nikki concurred. I then asked Tonya if she understood what Nikki was saying and if it was okay for her to take that stance.

Tonya: I understand, and it is okay.

Steven: (turning to Tonya) And do I understand that I am the only one to give coaching feedback?

I turned to Nikki and asked if she understood what Tonya was saying and was it okay. Nikki understood and said it was okay.

> Steven: So how can Nikki feel free to give input to the team and receive verbal support for her efforts so that Tonya can feel free of peer criticism and be respected?

Once both girls acknowledged their needs were valid, the brainstorming process began. Alternating, Nikki and Tonya offered solutions.

Nikki's solutions were not to coach Tonya; to support Tonya's efforts and suggestions; and to have her and Tonya pair up during partner drills. Tonya's solutions were to not speak in team huddles until everyone has a chance to talk, and to verbally encourage the team during practice and games. The girls agreed that they wanted to implement all of the solutions. They understood my wanting to pair them up only sometimes out of concern for the interaction that occurs among the team. The girls agreed to meet one week later to assess how their solutions were working and see if any adjustments needed to be made.

Conclusion: Since taking this class and implementing the principles with Nikki and Tonya, I can now see that the authoritarian approach is counterproductive and negatively impacts team chemistry. By facilitating the process, the girls were able to communicate their needs with a neutral party and have them validated by the other person. I was initially surprised that they didn't come up with solutions that the other would find disagreeable. However, after giving the process some thought, I came to the conclusion that the solutions suggested were reasonable and accepted because the girls first acknowledged the other's needs. Finally, my stress level remains low as the participants become the problem solvers.

What makes a person angry? He or she has suffered a loss. Here is where you make anger work in your favor. Angry people will tell you their loss; what's missing is their gain. Presto. Now you have the need for one side of the collaboration equation. By ameliorating feelings, you will have brought the parties to where they can be assertive with each other.

Aggressive postures do hinder effective communication, at least until a facilitator or moderator steps in to hear the anger, settle it, and uncover the underlying need. Aggressive behavior says, "You're stupid." Passive behavior suggests, "I'm stupid." Think of assertive behavior as neither passive nor aggressive. Forget the rule book on how to become assertive. Simply translate B's aggression into words that A can accept.

Again, one way to do this is to change from the active to the passive voice. For example, when Johnny says, "Sandra keeps teasing me," your response can be "You don't like being teased." Shifting to the passive voice keeps Sandra's name out of the picture temporarily, long enough for her to sit still with your statement. Remember—if Sandra erupts here, remind her that only one person can speak at a time.

Enforcing the Angry Rule

You can enforce the Angry Rule with any of the following:

- a hand held up to the offending party
- a reminder to the offending party about the Angry Rule
- the statement "I can't help you if both of you are talking at the same time"
- a threat to abort the process if they continue talking over one another
- the question "What would you like to happen now?"

Facilitators occupy a powerful position in the collaboration. Parties A and B do not want that power; it means the end of problem solving.

I have seen situations where the disputants willingly give power back to their facilitator, and I have even experienced it in a life-threatening moment in my own life.

Twenty years ago, I was jogging down Seattle's Queen Anne Hill when a youngster lying flat on his skateboard went flashing down through traffic, narrowly missing a car turning into his path. I instinctively grasped the arm of one of his less foolish friends as he tramped past and said, "Hey! Your friend could have been killed. Tell him don't skateboard on this hill." The young man jerked his arm away, and when I reached the bottom of the hill, the two of them blocked me in a vacant corner of a park. No one was there to witness as they jabbed their boards within inches of my face, threatening to kill me if I touched one of them again.

Foolishly, I tried to tough my way through the moment. I remembered a movie line Gene Hackman used to get out of a tight spot. I confronted the screamer with "You got a pretty good lawyer?"

"Yeah," he barked. "I got three of them, and they just got me out. Same as they'll do next time."

I couldn't dig myself in any deeper, so I went belly up. I sat on a rock abutment so they wouldn't see my knees shaking, and I asked, "What do you want to happen now?"

The situation immediately evaporated! The leader backed off, lowering his board. The other did the same, while chiming in absently, "We'll get you, old man" and "Don't you worry." They strode away, leaving me a confused bundle of nerves.

The truth of the matter is this: your conflict resolution will never get as far as my misadventure so long as you introduce a collaborative overlay in your classroom or school. In chapter 4, we will look at any number of interventions that can wisely take the place of collaboration. In the meantime, know that collaborating using a neutral third party facilitator is the last, best plan for those involved in a dispute. This is even truer when staff members are known to collaborate in smaller ways every day. By this time in your journey, everyone is watching—certainly the children in your school.

Collaborating without a Third-Party Facilitator

Guiding a collaboration while "owning" part of the problem is challenging. Nevertheless, experienced facilitators—those who have profited from experience as neutral mediators—will find they can conquer the situation without too much difficulty. The diagram below shows a schematic of how this facilitation might proceed, moving from full disclosure through hidden agenda and ending with conflict. Party A (or B) plays the facilitator.

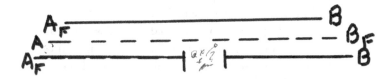

SIDEBAR

This diagram shows the more advanced training model where a neutral facilitator is not present. The role of 'F' must be played by the party with skills in that area, either A or B.

Once again, training in collaboration is designed to be incremental, developmental. This normally requires practice as a third party facilitator. It is a difficult way to learn because one's counterpart to the collaboration might view neutral behavior as a weakness. 'Changing hats' (between problem owner and facilitator) as Gordon called it is neither for the timid nor for the beginner.

In the following case study, teacher Charlene Ponsford describes a collaboration between herself and a fifth-grade student.

Situation: Brian would often come in from recess and yell put-downs at other students or call them cheaters.

This occurred in the first few days of school. At first, I just reminded Brian that put-downs are not allowed and that people do not like being called a cheater. However, this just didn't work. I asked Brian if he would see me after lunch to work out a solution to the problem.

Setting the Stage: I explained to Brian that we have a problem and that I would like to solve it in a way we would both feel good. Brian seemed to be relaxed with the suggestion. Both of us sat in a student desk facing each other. I leaned forward with paper and pen in hand. I then explained I had taken a class for teachers designed to help solve situations so that both people are happy with the outcome. I asked his permission to use the strategy. He replied, "Sure," gesturing with both hands, turning them over and open. This signaled to me his trust, so I felt good about proceeding. Oops—I forgot to ask if this is a good time and if he felt we had enough time.

Defining the Problem: I told Brian I wanted to write down our conversation because it was important and because we may need to look back on it later. I then told him that each of us will express our concerns around the situation, and then we would think about solutions. At the end we would pick those solutions we are both happy with. Brian responded with a confident "Okay."

> Charlene: Brian, I'll start first telling you what I need, and then I'll listen to what you need. Is that okay?
>
> Brian: Sure.
>
> Charlene: What I need is for the class to have no put-downs. It hurts peoples' feelings. You can understand that.
>
> Brian: I know.
>
> Charlene: So, Brian, what is your need? What do you want?
>
> Brian: Well, Jesse, Bubba, David, and Charles are cheating out at recess playing football.

Charlene: Ah, so I see now why you are so frustrated when you come in from recess. It's important to you that people are playing the game fairly or it's no fun.

Brian: Yeah, that's why I called Charles a cheater.

Charlene: So Charles is the problem?

Brian: Not so much as the other three. He only does it because other kids cheat. If they didn't cheat, Charles wouldn't.

Charlene: How are those other kids—Bubba, Jesse, and David—failing to play fairly?

Brian: When they have the ball and get touched, they keep on running.

Charlene: You mean they don't go down once they're tagged? They just keep on running even though the play is over? It bothers you that that's unfair.

Brian: Yup.

Charlene: Okay, Brian, your need is for fair play. When the boys get touched, they should go down and end the play.

Brian: Yes.

Needs Equation and Cross-Check:

Charlene: Is there anything you want to add?

Brian: No.

Charlene: Great! I think we have all the information. Before we begin to think of ways we can both get what we need, I want to be sure we understand each other's needs. Brian, do you understand and see why I have the need for no hurt feelings in our classroom?

Brian: Yeah, sure.

Charlene: Great! Your need is to have the others play fair football, going down when they are touched. I can understand your need.

Brian: Well, it's not all the time. Most of the time they play fair. It's just on some plays they cheat.

Charlene: Oh, okay, it's just sometimes.

Brian: Yeah.

Creative Solution: After brainstorming with Brian, we decided he would no longer use put-downs to solve his problem with recess. I would talk with the other boys' sixth-grade teacher, suggesting he say something like, "You boys are doing a pretty good job of playing football, but once in a while you are not ending the play when you are tagged. It would be better if you always went down when tagged." We agreed that Brian's name would be kept confidential because the older boys might turn on him. If unfair play continued, we could ask the principal to speak with the boys. If the problem still existed, we could expand the collaboration to include the other three boys.

Conclusion: It has only been two days, but there were no incidents. Brian is a troubled child with a difficult background. I'm not confident his outbursts will end, because Brian uses this behavior to cope. What did happen is Brian and I are building a trusting relationship where we can work to improve his coping skills. Brian felt important in our conversation. For me, I believe in this process. It allowed me to understand Brian's name-calling was not an attack on my authority, but a cry for help by a child with a need who doesn't know how to express it or fulfill it. We are all better off thanks to this process.

CHAPTER

4

SITUATIONAL LEADERSHIP
REVISITED

I was an oak. Now I'm a willow. I can bend.
—sung by Elvis Presley

Lao Tzu was no clairvoyant. When he wrote, "A leader is best when people barely know he exists," the ancient sage could not have anticipated the state of education today (Heider 1986). High-stakes testing challenges students while exhausting the system at the same time. On the one hand, charter schools are undermining the roots of public education. On the other, taxpayers demand accountability. Worse, Margaret Thatcher's enigmatic idea that "Consensus is the negation of leadership" has enough devotees to steer collaboration straight into the jaws of conflict (Thatcher 2005). Today, teachers find themselves with bull's-eyes on their backs, and leadership is as dizzying a task as they have ever faced. Hubris notwithstanding, the dean at a prominent teaching university offered this solution to his dilemma: "There is one way to lead around here. Mine!" (personal communication 2010).

Leadership! Socrates had trouble with it. So does Obama. Now, with charter schools, voucher programs, and right-wing interests like Eli Broad and the Koch brothers wanting a piece of the action, today's teacher faces tasks more capricious than most can imagine. Dredging up solutions is taxing. Implementing them is exhausting. Satisfying constituencies is improbable. Obtaining loyalty is hair-raising. Education is under siege.

Here are examples from our nation's schools: A principal appoints a committee, which ignites defiance. *You decide and tell us.* For trying to settle a difference among staff, a fellow teacher gets dissed. *You're not telling us who is right.* In a school where some thirty issues are unresolved, an entire staff grumbles about leadership by default. *We would never be in charge here. You couldn't pay us enough.*

What happens when a leader confronts her uncertain footing head-on? Principal Gerri Harmon was prudent about her new assignment, determined to be decisive right from the start. She paced her campus and then cut fifteen minutes off the working day. Were her teachers impressed? They filed a grievance overnight. "What's the difference?" she grimaces. "I'm doing what I did at my last school. These teachers will not let me take charge" (personal communication 2014).

Today there are many reasons why leading is different. Some of those factors—self-esteem training, assertiveness, and empowerment—were put in place by educators. Ironically, teachers must now oversee the boisterous free-for-all that results.

However, there is one other reason for the change that stands above the rest. In the years since Harmon passed a similar initiation in a nearby district, the hierarchy has flattened. Corporate America manipulated the flattening by slashing middle managers and plowing savings into the Bottom Line (Daft 2013). For teachers, this progression does not exist. For them, a flattened hierarchy means more than truncated chains of command. It means, suitably enough, that authority for authority's sake is dead. With independent expression encouraged, educators must listen, harmonize, and synthesize—all without resorting to power. Until we learn to do this, followers will continue to thrust forward ideas, but with little respect for the other guy's ideas. Nobody wants to be the leader, but everyone wants to lead.

Face to face with Harmon, and with no glib fix in mind, I started tentatively with, "You're hurt by this lack of support."

"Well, of course!" An anguished look unseated Harmon's cautious decorum. "I don't want control all the time," she pleaded. "I just want some control some of the time" (personal communication 2014).

With hierarchical models breaking down, many classroom teachers feel the same as Harmon. When do they need control, and how much control do they need? Bart Simpson comes alive in every classroom, and teachers must dance to his tune, balancing command and control with respect for the verbosity of every child.

Hersey/Blanchard: The Reigning Standard

For thirty years, the melding of authority with participative decision making has been the domain of Paul Hersey and Ken Blanchard, originators of a bell curve they called "situational leadership." Hersey and Blanchard argued that traditional leading, based on codes of accountability and the power to punish and reward, can be adjusted according to stages of group cohesion. The situational leader decides less as the subordinate group matures (Hersey 1984).

Situational leadership can be readily applied in schools. At many universities, Hersey and Blanchard's theory permeates graduate training for teachers and administrators. Small wonder! Group membership, finite work periods, the incremental nature of learning, independent tasks, the autonomy of teachers, and the learning needs of students—all are elements more patterned and more predictable than in the modern workplace. Schools would seem an ideal incubator for Hersey/Blanchard leading. In many cases, they are.

Yet, like the leading it promotes, Situational Leadership can itself be modified and adjusted to meet classroom realities. Hersey/Blanchard rests on internal measures: trust, bonding, knowledge, industry, and heart. Today, we can amplify it so that it recognizes forces acting upon the group as well as those within. In today's schools, where prerogatives reflects the insistence of corporations, parents, ethnic groups, politicians, and even self-assured moral voices, internal measures are not enough. Neither is it acceptable for leaders to subjectively assess their group's maturity. This *definitive* quality of leadership is what grates.

Moreover, leaders tend to have a preferred Blanchard style. "Research shows that 54 percent of leaders tend to use only one style, 35 percent tend to use only two styles, and a mere one percent use four styles" (Vistacampus.gov 2016)

Needed is a way to balance authority with participation, to meld group process leading with command and control. Yet as jurist Michael Josephson years ago lamented, "We stubbornly try to force authority to make some compromise with participation, and without success" (Josephson 1988).

Situational Leadership Revised

What happens when we chart leadership methods not according to group development but rather by the number of people who decide? If we accept Thomas Gordon's thesis that the terms *leadership* and *problem solving* are interchangeable, we pop through Alice's rabbit lair into uncharted landscapes indeed (Gordon 1977, 27). Just as there are many ways to solve problems, there are many ways to lead.

To match leader interventions with events, first create a spectrum or menu of styles (as in figure 1). Compromising, voting, commanding, collaborating, and consulting are all methods for deciding. Authority serves as the pole on the left, while 100 percent participation (for example, in jury deliberations) becomes the pole on the right.

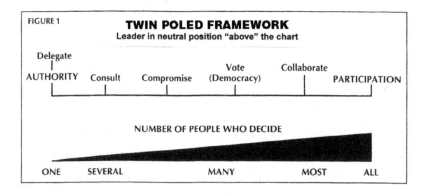

FIGURE 1

TWIN POLED FRAMEWORK
Leader in neutral position "above" the chart

Delegate

AUTHORITY   Consult   Compromise   Vote (Democracy)   Collaborate   PARTICIPATION

NUMBER OF PEOPLE WHO DECIDE

ONE   SEVERAL   MANY   MOST   ALL

By arranging leader interventions along the resulting chart, teachers can adjust their style to match events. Their behavior flexes with circumstances—perhaps shifting so rapidly that methods appear to overlap. Teacher Mary Shaw, for example, returned from recess to shouts from every fourth grader in her class. The use of the school basketball had triggered a dispute with another class. Mary opened the divider between classes (*decided*), supervised the choice of speakers (*voted*), and then facilitated (*mediated*) between factions. The two classes not only spoke through their delegates (*democracy*), they caucused (*consulted*) at times among themselves (personal communication 2013). Practiced flex leaders not only recognize these shifts, they foster them—and begin the delicate balance of participation with command and control.

The Role of Personal Values

Before teachers can adopt such a variable model, they may need a refresher in facilitation skills. However, they face a more daunting task—defining their essence as leaders. Faced with a multifaceted approach, teachers must determine which styles are compatible with their individual mind-sets and goals. As never before, they need to be clear about personal values.

Since teachers have different values, their individual menus will differ, becoming unique to the character and goals of each. While this precludes a universal leadership template, it also requires teachers to develop their own templates. Unlike bosses who stand on authority, today's educators must do nothing less than discover and then honor their own uniqueness.

To be proactive when choosing styles, teachers must have a grip on their values. For teachers to be recognized according to their dynamic along the chart (as opposed to how they wield authority), they need to put aside appearances and allow themselves to be known. Most teachers will be content with five or six favorite interventions. Once the menu pattern of the teacher becomes recognizable, energy and enthusiasm infuse the classroom and even the school.

Key Indicators: Impact and Concern

To guide flex leading among in-touch and vocal students, teachers will serve their interests by including one set of measures not found in Hersey/Blanchard: impact and concern. After decades of uneven reform in our nation's schools, *impact* and *concern* remain the hottest buttons in education. When pushed, they inflame entire communities, especially when decisions roll down from the top. They are the *hit* and *hurt* of modern leading.

Impact and concern will continue to transform teacher leadership. These two factors clamor for attention when decisions are made across the land. For example, to the question of who shall decide, we might ask: Who is affected? Who cares? Who has information we need? What degree of trust exists among the group? What priorities need attention?

How much time do we have? School reformers agree: to accomplish such alchemy, effective leadership begs to consider the concerns of those who put decisions to work.

When teachers consciously address these measures, the scope of their leading changes. The question is no longer how much authority to use, but rather, should authority be used at all? With which of many methods shall I intervene? These questions divide leadership into a two-step sequence, requiring teachers to first determine how a decision is to be reached. Because flex leading affects buy-in, matching leadership style with circumstance is more important than the wisdom of the actual decision. This is another way of saying that what is decided is not as important as all students accepting the solution and putting their shoulders to the wheel.

The Bipolar or Flex-Leader Option

In figure 1, teachers can select not from one style (authority) but from seven styles. Some are based on authority and some on participation. Since authority-based leading involves one decision-maker, the diagram shows authority on the left. Increasing the number of deciders moves the reader's imagination to the right. Of the disciplines shown, five are traditional. Pure participation is vague and, as such, problematic. Collaborative leading, despite much rhetoric, remains innovative. Because it has the structure lacking in random participation, collaborating becomes the *operative* pole on the right.

Adding styles now completes the framework—a menu ordered by the number of people who decide. Some styles are harder to place than others. Collaboration, for example, might be placed anywhere except at the pole on the left. In general, collaboration is a peer model of deciding that shuns authority and rank. Sometimes confused with collegiality or consensus, it is a process for *reaching* consensus. In general, two people can collaborate. So can an entire class. Since so many individuals might be involved, collaboration is shown nearer the pole on the right.

Once collaboration is decided upon, each teacher will begin to involve students based on specific values. Are the students affected? Are they concerned? Do students have information the teacher needs? Do students want a voice? Can students trust the others? Do they trust their teacher? Or does the teacher already have a solution in mind? Predetermined solutions spell trouble for would-be collaborators. Leaders who obscure their decision-making power while mouthing the jargon of collaboration have difficulty without equal, even among raw authoritarians. They place themselves at a high-risk position: top left along the chart (figure 2).

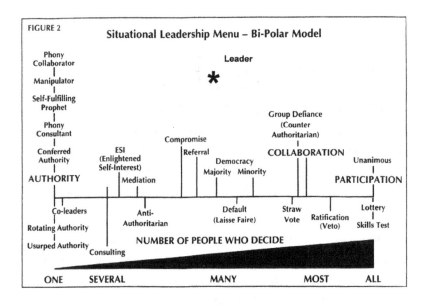

Trust for the Process

Trust for the process might come slowly. Where trust is present, children eagerly share solutions and ideas. Children are naturals here. They sense when to speak up, how to stay within the boundaries of each style, and when they are legitimately excluded from debate. Wonderfully prepared by decades of classroom innovation—assertiveness training, active listening, and self-esteem—children are ideally suited for the features of the twin-poled chart.

When teachers use the flex-leader model, the model itself generates trust. Trust increases regard for the model, resulting in reciprocity, just as with any mutual connection. In 2013, two years into flexible leading, Principal Lynn Roberts told me that she was astonished when two teachers asked to combine their curricula. "These two weren't even speaking with one another before we adopted the bi-polar model" (personal communication 2015).

"It's Under My Control"

Different teachers find different rewards. Flexible leading gives vice principal and school counselor Katherine Palmer a different reward—confidence. "I found a way to blend my two roles. It's okay to move from one end of the chart to the other. It's under my control" (personal communication 1996).

Beyond flexing among styles, implementing them is where miracles seem commonplace. In the classroom, teacher Raymond Salinas's collaboration resulted in students generating their own criteria for grading group presentations. Salinas reports:

> It's been a couple of days since my students devised their plan and implemented it. Watching my students has been refreshing. I see them working harder than normal, being more responsible for their learning, and having a better attitude for their work. Also, that work is much better than what it had been before. I notice a sense of pride. (personal communication 2010)

These educators did more than guide effective solutions. They transformed the construct of power in the classroom and provided a framework to resolve similar problems in the future.

Authority Here To Stay

For children to become effective leaders themselves, they need exposure to many leadership styles. By demonstrating from among some two dozen interventions (figure 2), teachers can show a reasonable complement of participatory methods without surrendering their authority. Indexing to one allows that authority-based leading has its place. Teachers reluctant to share power have their own integrity; they simply have different values.

With flex leading, no teacher needs to change. However, for men and women comfortable with authority, that fact may be best acknowledged. In today's world, acknowledging the tendency toward command and control may take more courage than learning new styles. Even so, as Abraham Maslow wrote, "many people assume that power in the form of strong leadership is always bad, overlooking the fact that there are healthy leaders whose motives are for the good of their organizations and for the good of society" (Goble 2004, 97). So, which will it be—authority-based leading or group-based leading? For decades, educators have been lost in limbo between the two, frustrating change and limiting reform.

The Not-So-Democratic Vote

As surreal as it seems, virtually all teachers already use a twin-poled model, with the pole on the right representing the democratic vote. However, voting fails the participation test for three reasons. First, it favors students who are articulate, sometimes forceful, and can think on their feet. Second, the minority has ultimate control of the result. When at odds with the outcome of the vote, all they must do is nothing. A simple majority may carry the day, but implementing tight voting becomes a heartless activity with more than its share of gripes.

Third, there is the impact and concern over questions like "Who is hit by this decision?" and "Who might this decision hurt?" These factors are often ignored when voting rises to the fore. After his class voted to keep their creative activities the same as the prior semester—reading, writing, and journaling in fifteen-minute segments—teacher Kevin Hoonan (1996, 28) tackled disruption from two middle school boys. After collaborating with his class, he determined that students could set their own priorities during the hour. Moreover, his students decided the former division of labor was not even worth considering. This overturned their ballot! Only moments before, repeating that course of action had been the outcome of their vote.

Teachers Setting Themselves Free

Blending impact and concern into leading is a straightforward process for teachers who spell out their values. Where competing theories require leaders to change—consider Stephen Covey's *7 Habits of Highly Effective People* or Donald Trump's *The Art of the Deal* —the flex-leader model invites them to become more authentic within themselves. Positioning oneself along the chart begins the moment leaders examine their values.

Flex leadership neither clarifies values nor raises skills. Rather, it provides a framework, a home for those tools. The result is color, vitality, flexibility, and a proactive dynamic—teachers choosing interventions, not feeling pushed and pulled by events. To reiterate, participatory management lets teachers become more of themselves, not less. Dr. Jon Kabat-Zinn, founder of the stress reduction clinic at the University of Massachusetts, writes, "It is impossible to become like somebody else. [To reduce stress] your only hope is to become more fully yourself" (1990, 36).

Rewards

Flex-leader rewards go beyond internal harmony and personal growth. With the model in place, teachers increase student ownership in solutions, ease implementation, lift self-esteem, nourish other esteem, raise achievement, and disarm student bickering. With flex leading, teachers revitalize parent support and soften the edge of administrators, governing agencies, and boards. Flex leading promises to brighten the classroom, stimulate creative thinking, and prepare children for their uniquely interactive future.

A Critical Juncture in Education

Despite studies critical of schooling, educators remain respected in their communities. Millions look to education, hungry for roles that bring citizens closer together and grown-ups closer to their kids. The public's objection to education reflects not so much a grievance as it does a forlorn hope.

As Barbara Cervone, a former teacher and current president of What Kids Can Do, argues, "Never before in the history of US education has there been so much talk about school reform. Like the dieter who tries one plan after another, schools have remained largely impervious to attempts to change their shape" (personal communication 2014). Converting to flex leading is not a quick fix—polishing skills, training staff, orienting parents, and coaching supervisory boards and community groups will take months, perhaps years. A task force member of the Institute for Educational Leadership explains:

> What we need is a partnership in which teachers are trained, encouraged, and required to be learners; where educators, legislators, and school board members are educated and informed about needs and issues, where everyone has a role to play, where there is no finger-pointing, where planning is collective, and where participants think outside the box together. (2001, 21)

Cervone continues, "A final element in good schools, often the ingredient that ties everything else together, is a collaborative approach to making decisions ... In schools that work, changes are not mandated, they are negotiated" (personal communication 2014). Collaboration can be the theme for the classroom, just as it can for the school environment. Yet even children know collaboration cannot be the only method. Among the scores of decisions teachers make daily, only some are amenable to a form of negotiated settlement. The safety of children plus the weight of time combine to legitimize authority when such is the chosen path.

The adventures of the 1990s taught us that while collaboration can be the theme, it cannot dominate the process. Time does not permit. A balance between authority and collaboration is required. This balance is where the Hersey/Blanchard model must finally bow to some form of group activity, leaving teachers with the ad hoc right to choose. Teachers can no longer control today's students, but they can control their sliding-scale spectrum, a product of their own design.

Meanwhile, "We've managed to take the fifteen years of children's lives that should be the most carefree, inquisitive, and memorable and fill them with a motley collection of stress and a neurotic fear of failure" (Gill 2012). Yet nowhere is the need larger, the emotions greater, nor the investment higher than when a shift in grown-up thinking affects the future of our kids.

Measuring Tools for Flex Leading

Flex leading corresponds to an index, as does Hersey/Blanchard leading. But for teachers locating themselves on the Hersey/Blanchard model, indexing involves descriptors internal to the group. This confines such teachers to authority, even if authority is practiced by degree. Flex leaders, on the other hand, add measures that are external to their group. Such measures are then ranked according to individual preference. This gives flex teachers a personalized values system, a lens through which to view the selection of styles. The resulting overlay applies to choosing methods, not solutions. For solution-finding, the values of the group come into play—unless, of course, the teacher chooses authority. In that case, the teacher's values have control throughout both the process and the solution.

In the chart below, the left column ranks my own values when I first began the Collaborative Center in 1984. (TCC was the nonprofit where I produced my collaboration workshops. It never received a grant and did not show a profit other than to open the doors to higher education, where I moved in 1991.) Thirty years of bipolar tinkering has meant personal growth and change for me—a point about which my friends occasionally agree. As a result, employees and students today are more likely to know me by the schedule on the right.

You might wonder why I chose these values or ranked them as I did, but that type of exercise is irrelevant. No one needs to comprehend your reasoning; people simply need to see what you believe in and observe you being consistent, especially as you flex between styles. Your standards and your consistency will become clear, and these will mark you as a leader.

The Author as Leader

Values (1984)		Values (Today)	
Policy		Safety	High
Safety		Impact	
Time		Concern	
Control (my need for)		Trust	W
Knowledge		Knowledge	E
Trust	Hersey/	Flexibility	I
Closeness	Blanchard	Closeness	G
Impact		Mood	H
Concern		Priorities	T
Mood (mine)		Policy	
Priorities		Time	
Flexibility		Control	Low

Think about what is important to you as you position yourself along the twin-poled chart. If you generally want accountability, you probably lean toward the left. If you prefer involvement, you lean toward the right. The job of teasing these general terms into detailed descriptors falls to each teacher. Look under the surface of the words. Does *involvement* mean connecting, bonding, fresh ideas, sharing responsibility, a sounding board? When you can list what you believe are the benefits of involvement, you will be looking in the direction of your values.

Even in bad light, insight into these values is not as timorous as I have made it appear. For example, although listing something like "keeping my job" might feel humbling, it is supported by enough human awareness to make Abraham Maslow proud, certainly in the current economy. Be honest about what drives you. Acknowledging your tendencies is crucial to being an effective leader. It helps students understand your leading and gets you thinking about your chart.

When it comes to influencing others, only phony participators (phony collaborators, manipulators, and phony consulters) have more trouble than the pure authoritarian. If you are not an authoritarian yet find that resistance is robbing you of confidence, it may be that you need to behave more intuitively and get proactive about this chart. The sense that the flex-leader menu is leading you may simply mean you are not leading it.

CHAPTER

5

MILLENNIAL CHILDREN AND NO CHILD LEFT BEHIND

A child miseducated is a child lost.
—John F. Kennedy

The decade-long thrust toward standardized testing has been a tragic error. In districts where children cannot compete, truancy and dropout rates have soared. States, realizing the cost of testing, are waiving and even reversing the requirements of No Child Left Behind. In recent years, state after state has demanded relief from its draconian demands. In Maryland, Montgomery County Superintendent Joshua Starr rejected NCLB funding, citing his district's nationally recognized evaluation system. He called for a three-year moratorium on standardized tests (Strauss 2012). Idaho, Montana, and South Dakota have threatened to ignore the law altogether (McNeil 2011). Testifying before congress, New York City teacher Jia Lee called NCLB a "great crime" (Lee 2015). Seattle Education Association President Jonathan Knapp categorically states that "Almost everything about No Child Left Behind is wrong" (personal conversation 2014).

It is not the tests as such that disturb kids. Teens I know say the tests are refreshing; they are a rush. It is the myopic focus on preparation that troubles educators and children alike. In the classroom, the pressure on teacher and child is intense. Berkeley professor David Kirp calls schools a "pressure cooker" and states that "students have become test-taking robots, sitting through as many as 20 standardized tests a year" (Kirp 2015, para. 5).

Everyone—teachers, parents, administrators, citizens, students—wants children to grow smarter. But we want them to grow emotionally and socially as well, and equally, during their hours in school. In the 1960s, Abraham Maslow decried "education which concerns itself with grades, credits and diplomas rather than wisdom, understanding and good judgment" (Hoffman 1988, 104). More recently, educator Mary Futrell writes, "The standards movement and the requirements of No Child Left Behind legislation made it abundantly clear: we can't simply set goals and then punish people for not achieving them" (Rubin 2009, xi).

Even prior to December 2015, an increasing number of parents had opted their children out of standardized tests, and they did so for many reasons, "including the stress they believe it brings on young students, discomfort with tests being used to gauge teacher performance, fear that corporate influence is overriding education and concern that test prep is narrowing curricula down to the minimum needed to pass an exam" (Zezima 2013, para. 2). Merrimack College Dean of Education Dan Butin adds that "assessments can never tell the full story of a child" (Butin 2012).

Finally, last December, Congress tackled the uproar created by its own law. Kentucky Senator Rand Paul spoke to repealing the law, stating that "many students have been failed by the current system" (Paul 2015). Senator Patty Murray, the ranking Democrat on the Senate's education committee, wrote that "NCLB has proved to be a deeply broken law with unrealistic requirements. It is hindering [teachers'] efforts and needs to be fixed" (Murray 2015).

The Problem with High-Stakes Tests

Here is the problem's nexus: The push toward standardized tests is more than a way to measure individual progress. It is also a way to hand out pass/fail grades to schools, thereby holding teachers accountable, but in only the single dimension of content. As 2012 National Superintendent of the Year Heath Morrison asks, "Why are we in a rush to do all this testing, then use it for accountability for schools and for accountability for teachers?" Morrison calls testing "an egregious waste of taxpayer dollars that won't help kids" (Helms 2012, para. 12).

Over and above the impediments to emotional and social growth, there are three things wrong with this approach. First, the grades handed to schools are a false litmus test for progress; damage is not being measured. While in cross-section, the 2015 dropout rate is lower, the United States high school *graduation* rate ranks in the bottom fourth of developed nations (OECD 2014). This is because in lower-income communities—home to so-called dropout factories—less than half the freshman class will graduate on time (Koebler 2011, para. 1). Children from these locales are the poor and minority children President Bush's education law was designed to assist (Hefling 2015). Yet more than eight thousand students leave formal schooling daily, most from impoverished communities (Statistic Brain 2014). So much for no child left behind. Education creates waves of youth left behind like the "Tune In, Turn On, Drop Out" druggie generation of the 1960s. Poor and minority youngsters are voting with their feet.

Second, education proceeds not just in math and reading, but also in breadth and depth. In the early days of the Bush administration,

Washington State's Commission on Student Learning met to hammer out standards for No Child Left Behind. I attended those meetings as an observer. Although commission members included district superintendents, most came from corporate America. Frederick Taylor, the father of time-and-motion studies—he introduced his method for force-feeding industrial production in 1881—would have been quite pleased. Taylor's effort was to standardize the nation's workforce by timing factory workers on their every move. Although scientific management (Taylorism) as a distinct theory was obsolete by the 1930s, most of its themes are still important parts of industrial management today (Eldritch Press 2013, para. 2).

The problem is, teachers are not industrialists. They want teaching to be about creativity, civics, and emotional development. They know and understand the in-depth growth that must take place in their charges. They are the professionals. They can be trusted to know schooling's larger purpose, whereas corporate executives cannot.

Standardization is not the answer. Frederick Taylor is simply another hawk for content. As educator and author Hank Rubin writes:

> Despite the fact that today, most schools continue to prepare young learners to be storage banks of knowledge and skills that they can summon on demand and exhibit on high stakes tests, we know that this type of accountability captures only a small portion of what we need from public education— and what today's and tomorrow's learners will need to succeed. (Rubin 2009, 26)

Seattle teacher Jesse Hagopian adds:

> I'm opposed to these tests because they narrow what education is supposed to be about and they lower kids' horizons. I think collaboration, imagination, critical thinking skills are all left off these tests and can't be

assessed by circling in A, B, C, or D. (Zezima 2013, para. 6)

Now we come to the third problem with the standardized-testing approach: it violates the military axiom that leaders dare not issue directives that cannot be enforced. The loss of respect is simply too great.

At Seattle's Garfield High School, January 9, 2014, was examination day. No kids showed up to be tested. The reason? No tests were set. Garfield teachers had earlier boycotted the exam, refusing to administer it. Saying the MAP (Measure of Academic Progress) test was flawed and students were sabotaging the outcomes because they knew the results made no difference in their grade, Garfield's staff unanimously determined to defy their district. There is no greater disrespect for leadership than to flout the leader's dictates. And there is no greater trepidation on the part of leaders than that a mandate of their own would reap mutiny and absolute disobedience.

Revolution in the Hood

Parents have also taken up the cudgel, willingly joining the acrimony over accountability. In Compton, California, hundreds of parent-protesters marched on Los Angeles education headquarters demanding a charter takeover of their neighborhood school. The Parent Revolution, which championed the McKinley School march under California's Parent Empowerment Act of 2010, heralded the action as if the French had again stormed the Bastille. The group called December 8, 2010, an historic day (McDonald 2010). Some two hundred schools—out of eight hundred—in the Los Angeles district had failed to meet No Child Left Behind standards (*Seattle Times* 2009), and as Parent Revolution chief Benjamin Austin says, apart from his revolution, "There is no consequence for failure and no reward for success" (Austin 2009).

So Austin would add another layer to the demand for accountability. In a demonstration of futility, California's so-called "trigger law," which granted takeover power to parents, was watered down "almost beyond recognition" by Julia Brownley, the chairwoman of the state's education committee. This weakening took place after Brownley allowed dozens of parents to testify about the importance of parent influence in their local schools. Brownley's version of the law meant failing schools would trigger nothing more than a "meaningless and patronizing hearing." The chairwoman announced her version with "great fanfare, *saying she had heard the call of the parents*" (Austin 2009; italics mine). In fact, Brownley flinched. She placed herself as a phony consulter, that high-risk position top left on the flex-leader chart. Outraged by Brownley's stance, McKinley's parents marched.

Deciding How to Decide

Arguably, a charter operator for McKinley Elementary might work as the parents anticipate. (The issue is moot. A legal technicality caused the parents' petition to be thrown out.) However, the outcome is not what matters here. It is the way things get decided that puts McKinley children at risk. Reports of threatened retribution and even physical provocation dotted the debate (Wilson 2011, 1). Even the word "revolution" seems overpowering. Inflamed rhetoric does nothing to further a good-faith caucus between educators, parents, the larger community, and the students themselves.

The McKinley charter has proven to be a nonstarter. But to carry on the debate in spiteful terms sets a dangerous precedent for McKinley's kids. They will learn about political power soon enough. They need a more creative solution now, while they are still innocent and can profit from a more collegial approach. Here, again, is Dr. Rubin:

The message of [my] book, *Collaborative Leadership*, is families, communities, educators, business leaders and policy makers are engaged in an ongoing relationship and share responsibility for the education of our children and youth. This teamwork ... deserves much more attention if we want to improve our schools and other public agencies to insure our children's future. (Rubin 2009, 42)

New Standards for a New Age

Rubin's "ongoing relationship" would require parties to abandon the Industrial Era anthem in which competition, not cooperation, guides the debate. Today's students are not growing up in the Industrial Age. They were not even born in it. Consider this list of desired characteristics of workers during the Industrial Era from Irving Burstiner. It was published near the end of that era, in 1984. In his classic but dated lament, Burstiner called for a revival of the following values:

- good level of productivity
- consistency
- honesty
- loyalty to the firm
- no rocking the boat
- pleasant personality
- promptness
- proper behavior on the job
- regular attendance
- respect for authority

What if the attributes of today's worker could connect with Burstiner's tenets while simultaneously replacing those values? For each of the 1984 bullets, a behavior characteristic of the Age of Information can be substituted. Keep in mind that today, no one person has enough information to make decisions in solitude—or even in consultation, which still smacks of solitude. For good level of productivity, one can substitute a good level of creativity. For consistency, contribution; for honesty, disclosure; for loyalty to the firm, loyalty to the process; for pleasant personality, effective personality; for no rocking the boat, rocking the boat; for promptness, results; for proper behavior, innovative behavior; for respect for authority, respect for ideas; and for regular attendance, total attendance.

Whatever Burstiner's intention, his characteristics no longer fit today's workplace, or even today's classroom. In fact, so long as content and accountability remain pivotal to school reform, corporate philanthropies like the Gates and Broad Foundations will continue to aggregate influence, districts will continue to circle the wagons, young people will continue to drop out, parents will continue to receive carefully vetted information, teachers will continue to be frustrated, and principals will continue to hold tight to the reins. No one can fault the administrator who says, "If my ship is going down, I will be the man at the helm." Yet together, these factors stifle collaboration, create winners and losers, and perpetuate the competitive mentality of an outmoded age.

The Phenomenon of Belonging

If one word could summarize the difference between the Industrial Age and the Age of Information, that word would be *belonging*. As it stands today, education is a closed community. It is closed to parents, and it is closed to children. There is significant debate as to whether it exists for children at all. Austin's League of Education Voters believes it exists for adults. Michelle Rhee, the ousted chancellor of the District of Columbia schools, echoes the league's position when she states, "Policy makers, district administrators, and school boards ... have created a bureaucracy that is focused on the adults instead of students" (Rhee

2010, 41). Belonging to the school community in anything more than a supporting role is rarely an option for children and families.

In one small Caribbean country, airport visitors are greeted with two large signs: *Belongers* and *Visitors.* As Pew Foundation Director Suzanne Morse writes, "The volumes written today about leadership fail to recognize the motivation and the necessity of belonging in leadership preparation and selection. The heart of leadership, 'belonging to a community and its common interest' is lost'" (2009, 7). All learning is rooted in the human need to feel a sense of belonging and of making a contribution to a community.

In our culture, there is evidence that children are positioned for belonging more than is commonly known. Why are they being denied? Once again, Maslow's hierarchy is revealing. Maslow distinguished between basic needs and what he called "meta" or growth, needs. In cross-section, basic needs have been provided through the prosperity of the Industrial Era. Still, for students to grow socially and emotionally, they must feel they belong. Among the needs that are commonly met prior to belonging, Maslow included self-esteem. Anyone who thinks children's self-esteem is not vital to a school culture should try mocking a child in the classroom. Action from the ACLU will follow close behind!

For three decades, the teaching of self-esteem has been pivotal to the school curriculum, creating a disconnect when it comes to incorporating children's voices in decision making. Children are prepared to assume a greater sense of belonging. In fact, they go to great lengths to belong— they simply do not include adults in their community.

In a collaborative environment, belonging becomes a reality. In Coeur d'Alene, Idaho, teacher Melita Clary collaborated with her kids over classroom rules. "Actually, I didn't need to give anything beyond my need for order," she writes. "If any idea went against my need, the rest of the children spoke out against it."

For Clary's students, cooperation was not the norm. Her new class had come to her with a reputation for being troublesome. After they collaborated, one girl came to her in tears and said, "You're the first teacher that gave our class a chance." Parents will not march on a collaborative school; their children will not allow it. (personal communication/written assignment 2004)

In fact, it is children who will remind us to collaborate. Author Charlotte Kasl describes a stalemate when her fourteen-year-old daughter wanted to see a movie and she was too sick to drive. After examining their mutual needs, they reached a solution together. When Kasl next faced a row with her daughter, the youngster pleaded, "Can it be like the time at the movies? Tell me the two sides" (1989, 271).

Clary, too, sometimes overlooks the chance to collaborate. She writes, "You can be sure the kids will remind me." Tom Gordon's own children have been known to force the issue. Once when Gordon was about to pronounce a decision, his daughter held up an index finger and mouthed "Method One," the win-lose method described earlier. Gordon quickly backtracked and asked what his daughter needed (Gordon 1977).

As junior high school teacher Gloria Tyler says, "When students partner with their teacher and are allowed to join in the decision-making process—even the teaching process—they begin to 'own' part of the classroom system. In that ownership, they become less disruptive, instead more relaxed and engaged learners" (personal communication 2014).

The Inadequacy of Authority

Why would teachers not look for alternatives to authority? Look at the factors that are being leveraged here. First, in education as in business, no single person has all the answers. Bosses who rely exclusively on the hierarchy of their position are routinely referred to as type A or micromanagers. To avoid the stigma, they hold meetings. Meetings that disregard the voices of subordinates lose the feedback that managers deeply need. Meetings that take place simply to announce a decision are a disaster—never more so than when the convener has positioned herself as having heard the peoples' concerns. As California's Julia Brownley learned, those only result in hostility and resentment.

Children need to prepare for a highly interconnected world. They need teachers who can listen and spark creativity. When it comes to classroom decision making, they need a genuine airing of ideas. And why not? Researcher Rensis Likert once noted that where there is more participation in management, the men at the top actually have more influence rather than less. "That is, the more influence and power you give to someone else in a team situation, the more you have to yourself" (Goble 2004, 20).

Second, there is the business of social media. Most of our young people use Facebook to exchange ideas with contemporaries across the country and even around the globe. The phenomenon has been the topic of much study, and its bonding element for young people has been described. Our children are simply accustomed to connecting— uniting on a genuinely intimate level. They need the same from their schooling. We should also not overlook the fact that in many cases, they gain a degree of intimacy, of togetherness. The tipping point remains at a distance before all children enjoy the fruits of collaborative teaching, learning, and deciding.

Third, the industrial hierarchy has collapsed. Apart from military and paramilitary organizations, command and control has done nothing to redeem itself since Harvard's Rosabeth Moss Kanter predicted that the hierarchy would collapse of its own weight. Kanter (1990) likened the world of global competition to a corporate Olympics. The winners in these "games" would be nonhierarchical, cooperative, and focused on processes, the way things are done. They would also, she said, have a dose of humility.

The flattening of the hierarchy that took place in the '90s was designed to create a more streamlined organization. It did that. But it also riffed midlevel managers and doubled the workload of those who stayed behind. Today, there are even books about bottom-up leadership—for example, *How to Manage Your Manager* and *Followership: How Followers Are Creating Change and Changing Leaders.* Understandably, top-down management has lost much of its cachet.

Fourth, there is the Bart Simpson effect: our kids believe they can say anything that comes to mind. Thanks to many years of applied psychology in our nation's schools, children have become remarkably in touch with their inner musings—and eager to let everyone know what those are. The result is children who are more than outspoken; they believe their every notion *must* be aired. No wonder they clamor for collaboration once they have tried it out.

Fifth is the business of self-esteem. Unlike most adults, today's kids were not raised in a culture of sin, guilt, and redemption (Leins 2015). They do not comprehend it. Their esteem will not allow it. A function of applied psychology that has informed teaching for the past thirty years, the esteem movement will never reverse itself. It is here to impact us … well, forever. What that means is children not only gushing with ideas but also seeing their ideas as necessary to the outcome of any event.

Finally, there is the Information Age. The Age of Industry has passed, leaving a legacy of triumph and domination that is being eroded by a global economy, one that sees goods produced abroad. The US economy is based on service, which in turn involves the sharing of information. This may seem trite; most of us know about this shift already. Still, it is a factor in education because today's youth know nothing of the heyday of industrial life. In particular, they know little of the exponential growth that marked the economic wave following

World War II. They only know about their laptops, their iPads, their tablets, and the information to be found there—all of it made to be shared.

Taken together, corporate connectivity, social networking, the demise of the hierarchy, children's verbosity, the self-esteem movement, and the reality of the Information Age all point to collaboration as the way out of education's abyss. While the above items might seem enigmatic and a problem to some, they can also be looked at as the ingredients for a collaborative educational culture. Yes, taken separately, they might seem problematic. Taken together, they might simply describe the detritus of an industrial era and the top-down leader model that it brought to bear.

Giving Participation Another Chance

Today we are at a crossroads. The Human Potential Movement of the 1990s failed. It failed because of resistance to viewing humans as our greatest underdeveloped strength. The human being remains an untapped asset. But what does that mean in the face of how teachers teach? It means little more than an invitation, a plea for a second chance.

Collaborative endeavor stands like the proverbial low-hanging fruit. The main ingredients are present—the attending skills of teachers and the exuberance of kids—and the cost is nothing save a few minutes away from test prep and standardized content. All that is needed is the support of administrators and parents … and patience on the part of the corporate agenda.

Summary

Education's cast of characters has changed. Once teachers were the workers, principals the managers, children the raw material (and eventual product), and industry the consumer. In today's world, the divisions are far more complex. Children and teachers together are the workers. Curriculum, books, and experiences are the raw materials. Kids' creativity and ideas are the product, and the consumer is an entire society.

Most important, education's investors were formerly the parents. Now students do the investing—and many of today's youth are withdrawing their equity. Rather than face a classroom where they feel they do not belong, they are opting for low-paying jobs and the tedious need to live at home. They are simply not willing to be judged on their ability to stockpile knowledge and vomit it up on high-stakes tests. If that's all education is about, they are willing to risk a future life on the streets.

It is said that teachers make scores of decisions every day, striving to solve classroom problems that occupy part of each day's labor. Children are prepared to take part in those outcomes, at least on occasion and to an extent. They are being blocked by time-intensive test prep and the teacher's vested interest in command and control. Collaborative leadership offers a path that educators can follow to bring out the healthy values of today's kids and give them a sense of belonging to something greater than themselves. It can provide the social bonding that keeps children enthusiastic and keeps our youth in school.

EPILOGUE

Because relationships are at the core of collaboration,
an easy case can be made that the most important
public context for doing collaboration is in and
around our public schools.
—Hank Rubin

One might argue that the most important public context for collaboration is in Washington, DC. But let's get real. Adversarial politics gets in the way of collaborative deciding.

Yet it is notable that Congress, as of December 2015, showed uncommon unanimity in returning No Child Left Behind to the states. The federal government is finished with micromanaging education. It will be interesting to see if under the reign of President Trump, such bipartisanship lasts.

It bears pointing out that our children's education will likely remain under state oversight. *That* will certainly last. Federal government interference with our children was based on Texas's unproven model, and for fourteen years the boondoggle has left a legacy of negativity toward our schools on the part of adults and children alike. No one dares ask if the violence in education is a product of an atmosphere of overwhelm, hostility, and resentment—a culture of punitive indifference.

On December 10, 2015, President Obama announced the failure of No Child Left Behind together with the demise of his own Race to the Top. According to the laws of scientific experiment, trying and failing *do* represent an advance. That is because the trial doesn't have to be repeated. But here, the Law of Unintended Consequences has to include a generation of kids struggling to understand. That they are so adept, and so enamored with the collaborative method, must leave them wondering what happened to their formative years. From athletes to musicians to husbands and wives, no one ever achieved when external pressures forced them to perform beyond what they could comprehend.

I'll say this for No Child Left Behind: testing is good. It gives us a yardstick with which to measure individual progress as well as a point of international comparison with students abroad. Children expect to be tested. Teachers expect to be evaluated. But no test has ever measured a child's focus—that head-in-the-game, giving in excess of 100 percent—as competently as teachers, who are schooled in doing exactly that. It was the uber testing, the myopic focus on excessive tests to both gauge student progress and evaluate teacher effectiveness, that frustrated lawmakers, administrators, staff, and students alike.

With the states retaking oversight of education, this is an interesting time to try something new. It cannot be a repeat of the decentralized deciding of the '90s, however. Unguided caucuses, whether at the classroom or the school level, only result in time-consuming gripe sessions.

This time, let's make it a genuine experiment, not one with a foregone conclusion, such as "100 percent of students will perform at grade level," as the 2002 law decreed. If states are truly committed to "replacing some drill-and-kill memorization with more hands-on learning and critical thinking," then collaborative deciding—equating the needs of student and teacher—would seem an enticing place to begin (Kirp 2015). Switching to a collaborative climate in place of command and control will require courage on the part of principal and staff. But the resulting school culture promises to be a place of vitality and excitement rather than fear and loathing. As that happens, we will all be glad to "consign No Child Left Behind to the dustbin of history" (Kirp 2015, para. 1).

REFERENCES

Anderson, P. 1990. *Great Quotes from Great Leaders*. Lombard, IL: Successories Publishing.

Armario, C. 2011. "Other States Joining Idaho Defying No Child Left Behind Requirements." *Seattle Times*, July 21.

Austin, B. 2009. "Put Power Over California's Schools in Hands of Parents." *Los Angeles Times*. December 16. http://articles.latimes.com/print/2009/dec/16/opinion/la-oe-austin16-2009dec16.

Butin, D. 2012. "Arm Teachers! A Response to the NRA." *Huffington Post*. December 21. http://www.huffingtonpost.com/dan-w-butin/arm-teachers-a-response-t_b_2349845.htmlCharlotte.

Covey, S. 1989. *The 7 Habits of Highly Effective People*. Kindle Edition.

Daft, R. L. 2013. *Organizational Theory and Design*, 11th ed. Mason, OH: Cengage Learning.

Eldritch Press. 2013. "Frederick Winslow Taylor." ibiblio.org. http://www.ibiblio.org/eldritch/fwt/taylor.html.

Fisher, R., and W. Ury. 1981. *Getting to Yes: Negotiating Agreement Without Giving In*. Boston/New York: Houghton Mifflin Company.

Gill, A. A. 2012. "Schools Are Ruining Our Kids." *Vanity Fair*. December. http://www.vanityfair.com/culture/2012/12/aa-gill-schools-ruining-our-kids.

Goble, F. 2004. *The Third Force*. Chapel Hill, NC: Maurice Bassett Publishing.

Gordon, T. 1974 *Teacher Effectiveness Training*, New York: Random House.

————. 1977. *Leader Effectiveness Training*, 1ˢᵗ ed. New York: Wyden Books.

Greenleaf, R. 2015. *What Is Servant Leadership?* https://greenleaf.org/what-is-servant-leadership/.

Hefling, K. 2015. "Too Much Testing in Schools? Senate Panel Considers Changes." January 21. Associated Press.

Heider, J. 1986. *The Tao of Leadership*. Kindle edition.

Helms, A. 2012. "New State Tests Waste Tax Dollars." *Charlotte Observer*, December 27. http://www.journalnow.com/news/state_region/charlotte-superintendent-new-state-tests-waste-tax-dollars/article_47bd50c6-4b6e-11e2-8a1d-0019bb30f31a.html.

Hersey, P. 1984. *The Situational Leader*. New York: Warner Books.

Hoffman, E. 1988. *Maslow: The Right to Be Human*. New York: Tarcher/Penguin Books.

Holmes, O. W. Jr. 1919. Retrieved from http://www.answers.com/Q/Who_said_The_right_to_swing_your_arm_ends_when_the_other_persons_nose_begins.

Hoonan, K. 1996. "Collaborating with the Middle School Classroom." *Emergency Librarian* 23 (3).

Institute for Educational Leadership. 2001. "Redefining the Teacher as Leader." *Schools for the 21ˢᵗ Century Annual Report*, April: 21.

Josephson, M. 1988. *A World of Ideas*, interview with Bill Moyers. PBS TV.

Kabat-Zinn, J. 1990. *Full Catastrophe Living*. New York: Delacorte Press.

Kanter, R. M. 1990. *When Giants Learn to Dance*. New York: Routledge.

Kasl, C. 1989. *Women, Sex, and Addiction; A Search for Love and Power*. New York: Harper & Row.

Kellerman, B. 2010. *Leadership: Essential Selections on Power, Authority, and Influence*. New York: McGraw Hill.

————. 2012. *The End of Leadership*. New York: Harper Collins.

Kirp, D. 2015. "Left Behind No Longer: Why the New Education Law Is Good for Children Left Behind. *New York Times*, December 10. http://www.nytimes.com/2015/12/10/opinion/why-the-new-education-law-is-good-for-children-left-behind.html?ref=topics.

Koebler, J. 2011. "How to Identify a High School Dropout Factory." *US News and World Report*, November 30. http://www.usnews.com/education/blogs/high-school-notes/2011/11/30/how-to-identify-a-high-school-dropout-factory.

Lee, J. 2015. "Senate Hearings Reauthorization of NCLB." https://dianeravitch.net/2015/01/21/in-senate-hearings-on-nclb-lamar-alexander-quotes-carol-burris/.

Leins, C. 2015. "Americans Becoming Less Religious Thanks to Millennials." *US News and World Report*, November 3. http://www.msn.com/en-us/news/us/americans-becoming-less-religious-thanks-to-millennials/ar-BBmNSus?li=BBgzzfc&ocid=U146D.

MacGregor, D. 2010. "Theories X and Y, Revisited." *Oxford Leadership Journal* 1, no. 3 (June). http://www.oxfordleadership.com/journal/vol1_issue3/stewart.pdf.

Maslow, A. 2015. *Toward a Psychology of Being*. http://www.envisionsoftware.com/articles/Maslows_Needs_Hierarchy.html.

McDonald, P. R. 2010. "Compton Parents Petition to Take Over Chronically Failing Public School Through 'Parent Trigger' Law, Send Shock Waves Throughout the Nation." *LA Weekly*, December 8. http://www.laweekly.com/news/compton-parents-petition-to-take-over-chronically-failing-public-school-through-parent-trigger-law-send-shock-waves-throughout-the-nation-2393224.

McNeil, M. 2011. "More States Defiant on NCLB Compliance." *Education Week Spotlight*.

MetLife Foundation. 2010. "Survey of the American Teacher." https://www.metlife.com/assets/cao/contributions/foundation/american-teacher/MetLife_Teacher_Survey_2010.pdf.

Mill, J. S. 1859. *On Liberty*. Retrieved from http://oll.libertyfund.org/quote/201.

Morse, S. 2009. "New Metaphors for Leadership." *Civic Partners,* annual report of the Pew Foundation.

Murray, P. 2015. "Congress Needs to Fix Outdated Federal No Child Left Behind Education Law." *Seattle Times*, January 22.

Organization for Economic Cooperation and Development (OECD). 2014. Aneki.com. http://www.aneki.com/oecd_countries_high_school_graduation_rates.html?number=25.

Paul, R. 2015. *Town News Online*, January 29.

Piercey, D. 2010. "Why Don't Teachers Collaborate? A Leadership Conundrum." *Phi Delta Kappan Magazine* 92 (1).

Rhee, M. 2010. "What I've Learned." *Newsweek*, December 13.

Rubin, H. 2009. *Collaborative Leadership*. Thousand Oaks, CA: Corwin/Sage.

Seattle Times staff. 2009. "Los Angeles School District Hopes Charter Approach Rescues Failing Schools." *Seattle Times*, August 30. http://www.seattletimes.com/opinion/los-angeles-school-district-hopes-charter-approach-rescues-failing-schools/.

Statistic Brain. 2014. http://www.statisticbrain.com/high-school-dropout-statistics/.

Strauss, V. 2012. "Montgomery County Schools Chief Calls for Three-Year Moratorium on Standardized Testing." *Washington Post*, December 10. http://www.washingtonpost.com/blogs/answer-sheet/wp/2012/12/10/moco-schools-chief-calls-for-three-year-moratorium-on-standardized-testing/.

Thatcher, M. 2005. Extreme Wisdom. http://extremewisdom.blogs.com/extremewisdom/2005/04/consensus_is_th.html.

Trump, D. 1987. *The Art of the Deal.* New York, N.Y. Random House.

Vistacampus.gov. 2016, "Situational Leadership" p. 8a https://www. vistacampus.gov/sites/default/files/legacy/50/Training/ TrainingResources/LeadershipTrainingModule/situational_ leadership.pdf

Wilson, S. 2011. "Pulling the Trigger on Failing Schools." *LA Weekly,* December 1. http://www.laweekly.com/news/ pulling-the-trigger-on-failing-schools-2173138.

Woodbury, S. 2014. "Life Expectancy in the Middle Ages." http://www. sarahwoodbury.com/life-expectancy-in-the-middle-ages/.

Zezima, K. 2013. "More Parents Opting Kids Out of Standardized Tests." *MPR News,* September 8. http://www.mprnews.org/story/2013/09/08/ education/parents-opting-kids-out-of-standardized-tests.

Zuckert, C. 2014. "Machiavelli and the End of Nobility in Politics." *Social Research: An International Quarterly* 81, no. 1 (Spring 2014). https://muse.jhu.edu/article/543793/pdf.

APPENDIX 1

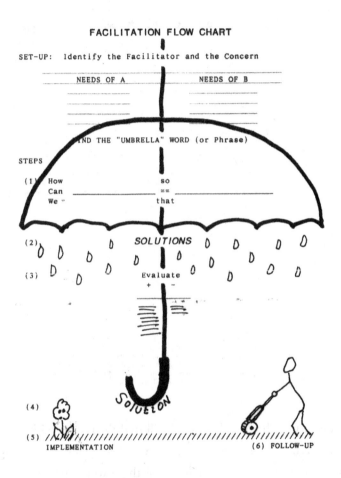

FACILITATION FLOW CHART

SET-UP: Identify the Facilitator and the Concern

NEEDS OF A   NEEDS OF B

FIND THE "UMBRELLA" WORD (or Phrase)

STEPS

(1) How   so
    Can   ==
    We   that

(2) SOLUTIONS

(3) Evaluate
    +   −

(4)

SOLUTION

(5) IMPLEMENTATION   (6) FOLLOW-UP

Reproducible: For teachers to track their own
collaborations as they move along.

APPENDIX 2

 ## AUTHORITY BASE

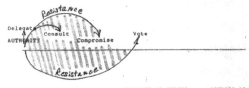

© Center for Collaboration and Teamwork
12/89 (Revised, January 1993)

Teachers using the bi-polar model will find themselves with as few as two and as many as five or six favored styles, seldom more. This diagram lists the advantages and limitations of those whose preferred base is authority. The term 'base' simply means the option of first refusal -- nothing is negotiable except situations which demand to be negotiated. Authority-based teachers should expect resistance to direct them to alternate styles, as indicated by the schematic.

Teachers using the bi-polar model will find themselves with as few as two and as many as five or six favored styles, seldom more. This diagram lists the advantages and limitations of those whose preferred base is authority. The term 'base' simply means the option of first refusal -- nothing is negotiable except situations which demand to be negotiated. Authority-based teachers should expect resistance to direct them to alternate styles, as indicated by the schematic.

APPENDIX 3

COLLABORATION BASE

AUTHORITY — Compromise — Vote — COLLABORATION — PARTICIPATION

Invitation *Invitation* *Invitation* *Invitation*

SOURCES OF STRESS:

Time
New Learning
Non-Conforming
Adjustment

SOURCES OF SATISFACTION:

Community
Morale
Good Solutions
Growth

For teachers based in collaboration, everything is negotiable except that which proves otherwise. Here the teacher/leader will be coaxed by invitation to the more economical style. Regardless of which pole the leader chooses as a 'base,' s/he does not give up the neutral position atop the chart.

Somewhat derisively, Tom Gordon once said leaders spend 20 percent of their time solving problems; another 20 percent of the time there are no problems. The remaining 60 percent of the time leaders go around solving problems that do not exist. Translated into education, imagine teachers having 80 percent of their time available for teaching.

For teachers based in collaboration, everything is negotiable except that which proves otherwise. Here the teacher/leader will be coaxed by invitation to the more economical style. Regardless of which pole the leader chooses as a 'base,' s/he does not give up the neutral position atop the chart.

Somewhat derisively, Tom Gordon once said leaders spend 20 percent of their time solving problems; another 20 percent of the time there are no problems. The remaining 60 percent of the time leaders go around solving problems that do not exist. Translated into education, imagine teachers having 80 percent of their time available for teaching.

APPENDIX 4

A Mock-Up of the Garfield
MAP Settlement through Collaboration

Leader Jesse Hagopian and the Garfield staff won a Pyrrhic victory over the administration when the Seattle Superintendent handed down his own solution: the MAP test (Measure of Academic Progress) would continue, and all standardized exams would be evaluated at the end of the 2014 school year. The cost of that decision was high. Superintendent Jose Banda resigned. He had been the subject of a costly executive search and had spent less than two years on the job, only to leave for greener pastures in the wake of the nationally publicized dispute. Here is an example of decisions being forged out of conflicting positions.

An effective collaboration would have looked something like this: A facilitator would have introduced the topic to participants Hagopian and Banda. A typical setup would have been performed to gain acceptance of the process and reinforce commitment to the result. The needs assessment might have contained the need of Banda to keep federal money flowing into the district. Hagopian describes his own need as eliminating meaningless testing, which would likely have parsed into returning to the task of teaching. Following the cross-check for both understanding and commitment, the actual collaborative equation might have resembled: *How can we keep the district fiscally stable so that we get more teaching time for the staff?*

I do not suggest an easy answer. Likely the result would have been exactly what the superintendent decided. However, at issue here is not just the outcome; it's how things get decided that adds harmony to the environment and mutual support for the result. It is people deciding solutions together that ultimately carries the day. And needless to say, evaluating standardized testing would take a more positive turn had it been the conclusion of a successful collaboration, not just an edict of the boss.

ABOUT THE AUTHOR

Don Broadwell began teaching collaborative leadership in 1984 after a career counselor advised him to shed the authoritarian style he had learned in the Marine Corps. Following grad school and a six-year stint with the Marines (in reverse order), Don spent a career in sales, supplying library books to schools. He retired from sales after forty years but continues to train teachers on nights and weekends, as he has for the past three decades.

Don's CV includes an undergraduate degree in mathematics and a Princeton Theological Seminary degree in pastoral counseling. As an adjunct instructor, Don has taught for the University of Idaho (Coeur d'Alene), Seattle Pacific University, Antioch University (Seattle), and Green River College (also in the Seattle area). He directs the Collaborative Center in suburban Maple Valley, Washington. His breakout workshops for national conferences include the Association of Experiential Education and the Association of Federally Employed Women. Don can be reached at donbroadwell@the-collaborative-center.org or by contacting the publisher.

ABOUT THE BOOK

Review and Endorsement
October 3, 2016

Don Broadwell (2016), Collaborative <u>Leadership for Classroom and School</u>

<u>Rebecca Olness</u>

"Don leads the reader through classroom examples of balancing authority with collaboration and, most importantly, how a sense of belonging leads to achievement and connectivity. Both new and seasoned teachers will benefit from reading and implementing strategies outlined in this book."

Rebecca Olness, MEd. is a retired educator, literacy consultant and former Board Member of the International Reading Association. She has presented on leadership and literacy skills in the United States, Canada, Europe, New Zealand and the Caribbean and is the author of two books on the topic.

<u>Lyon Terry</u>

"This book is essential reading for teachers, especially new teachers who will have hundreds of problems to solve every day. Don Broadwell gives a clearly laid out problem-solving methodology for teachers and leaders of all types."

Lyon Terry, MEd, NBCT, teaches 4th grade at Lawton Elementary in Seattle. He is the 2015 Washington State Teacher of the Year.

John Okerman

"Powerful and compelling, Don Broadwell has addressed the major challenges students and teachers confront daily. Collaborative Leadership for Classroom and School offers a path that educators can follow to bring out the healthy values of today's children and give them a sense of belonging to something greater than themselves. Don demonstrates authority and collaboration are both starting places for leaders and can be used simultaneously. It's not another "one style fits all"! An outstanding example of research, scholarship, and analysis, this book should not only be used by educators but is extremely relevant to business, industry, and governmental organizations."

John Okerman, Teacher, vice principal, Colonel, USMC (Ret.)

Printed in the United States
By Bookmasters